The Baptist
Confession of Faith
&
The Baptist Catechism

The Baptist
Confession of Faith
&
The Baptist Catechism

Solid Ground Christian Books
Port St. Lucie, Florida USA

Solid Ground Christian Books
1682 SW Pancoast Street
Port St. Lucie, FL 34987
205-587-4480
www.solid-ground-books.com
email: mike.sgcb@gmail.com

First Printing of Hardcover Bonded-Leather Edition June 2010
ISBN: 978-1-59925-245-2

First Printing of Flexible Bonded-Leather Edition November 2014
ISBN: 978-1-59925-346-6

First Printing of New Paperback Edition November 2014
ISBN: 978-1-59925-347-3

Second Printing of Hardcover Bonded-Leather Edition February 2018
ISBN: 978-1-59925-245-2

Second Printing of the Paperback Edition February 2018
ISBN: 978-159925-377-0

PRINTED IN THE UNITED STATES OF AMERICA

TABLE OF CONTENTS

FOREWORD
James M. Renihan

In February, 1694, a new congregation, known as the Maze Pond Church from their location in the city, was constituted in London. The very first page of their manuscript church book begins with these words:

> We believe the holy Scriptures of the old and new testament to be the word of God, and a sufficient rule of all saving knowledge, faith and obedience, further herein we agree with a Confession put forth by our brethren the Baptists in the year 1688 and signed at a General assembly by thirty seven of them.

Their intent in stating this was very simple. For this church, the *Second London Baptist Confession* defined their theological identity. And they were not alone. The thirty seven 'brethren' mentioned were merely representative of over 100 churches in England and Wales which held the Confession in high esteem. Soon after, it crossed the Atlantic Ocean, and became the theological standard for most Baptist churches in the American colonies, known in the north as the *Philadelphia Confession* (it was originally printed in Philadelphia by Benjamin Franklin) and in the south as the *Charleston Confession*. It is widely recognized as the most important Baptist Confession written in the English language.

We do not know all of the details about the first appearance of this Confession. Though it is commonly called the '*1689* Confession', it was actually first printed in *1677*. The title page for that original edition states that it was 'put forth by the elders and brethren of many congregations of Christians (baptized upon profession of their faith) in London and the Country.' While some have read this and assumed it indicates a general meeting of representatives of the churches in 1677, this is highly unlikely and almost certainly not correct. There is no extant record in any source hinting at such a meeting, and political pressures in that year would have been prohibitive. It more likely refers simply to the circulation and adoption of the Confession among a large number of churches throughout the country. The 1677 edition was unlicensed by the political authorities, contains no printing data beyond the year, and carries all the hallmarks of an underground enterprise. It almost certainly was a surreptitious publication.

For this reason, it is difficult to pinpoint the time of year when it came from the printer. The first known reference to the Confession is in the manuscript church book of London's Petty France congregation. In that book we read that on August 26, 1677, this note was entered: 'It was agreed that a Confession of faith, with the Appendix thereto having been read and considered by the Brethren: should be published.' This indicates a publication date later in the year, and may also point to the source and editors of the Confession: the Petty France Church and its pastors Nehemiah Coxe and William Collins. These two men were held in high esteem by their peers, Coxe being the son of the Baptist pioneer Benjamin Coxe, and Collins a divinity graduate of one of the Universities (we don't know which one). It seems likely that they edited a variety of documents, produced the Confession, presented it to their church for approval, and then circulated it among other congregations. Certainly it was well received and adopted by others, becoming the standard for their churches.

What documents were used in editing the Confession? I imagine a scene like this: on a table is placed an English Bible, a Hebrew Old Testament, a Greek New Testament, copies of the *Confession of Faith* as well as the *Larger* and *Shorter Catechisms* of the Presbyterian Westminster Assembly of 1643–48, the *Savoy Declaration* and *Platform of Polity* produced by the Congregationalists who met at the Savoy in London in 1658, and a copy of the *First London Baptist Confession* of 1646. Perhaps there were other books on that table also. But certainly, the editors employed each of these in thinking through and expressing the system of Christian theology they bequeathed to us.

Strangely, there is no bibliographic evidence to indicate that it was ever printed in 1689. We know certainly that it was printed in 1677, 1688 and 1699. The 1689 date derives from its adoption at the London General Assembly of the Particular Baptist churches.

This new edition of the Confession restores the document to its original state. Few realize that the earliest editions included, not just the text of the 32 chapters, but also an irenic epistle 'To the Reader' which provides some historical and theological context for the original version, and an Appendix on baptism, briefly explaining the rationale for the Baptists' rejection of paedobaptism and advocacy of credobaptism. For years, I have been convinced that this supporting material ought always to be included—and now thankfully it is.

It is a delight to send forth this leather bound edition of one of the great theological statements of Baptist history. May the Lord use it powerfully for the furtherance of his kingdom.

James M. Renihan
Escondido, CA
May 2010

TO THE JUDICIOUS AND IMPARTIAL READER

Courteous Reader: It is now many years since divers of us (with other sober Christians then living, and walking in the way of the Lord, that we profess) did conceive ourselves to be under a necessity of publishing a Confession of our Faith, for the information and satisfaction of those that did not thoroughly understand what our principles were, or had entertained prejudices against our profession, by reason of the strange representation of them by some men of note who had taken very wrong measures, and accordingly led others into misapprehension of us and them. And this was first put forth about the year 1643, in the name of seven congregations then gathered in London; since which time divers impressions thereof have been dispersed abroad, and our end proposed in good measure answered, inasmuch as many (and some of those men eminent both for piety and learning) were thereby satisfied that we were no way guilty of those heterodoxies and fundamental errors which had too frequently been charged upon us without ground or occasion given on our part.

And forasmuch as that Confession is not now commonly to be had, and also that many others have since embraced the same truth which is owned therein, it was judged necessary by us to join together in giving a testimony to the world of our firm adhering to those wholesome principles by the publication of this which is now in your hand. And forasmuch as our method and manner of expressing our sentiments in this doth vary from the former (although the substance of this matter is the same), we shall freely impart to you the reason and occasion thereof. One thing that greatly prevailed with us to undertake this work was (not only to give a full account of ourselves to those Christians that differ from us about the subject of baptism, but also) the profit that might from thence arise unto those that have any account of our labors in their instruction and establishment in the great truths of the Gospel, in the clear understanding and steady belief of which our comfortable walking with God, and fruitfulness before Him in all our ways, is most nearly concerned; and therefore we did conclude it necessary to express ourselves the more fully and distinctly; and also to fix on such a method as might be most comprehensive of those things we designed to explain our sense and belief of; and finding no defect in this regard in that fixed on by the Assembly, and, after them by those of the congregational way, we did readily conclude it best to retain the same order in our present Confession; and also when we observed that those last mentioned did in their Confessions (for reasons which seemed of weight both to themselves and others) choose not only to express their mind in words concurrent with the former in sense concerning all those articles wherein they were agreed, but also for the most part without any variation of the terms, we did in like manner conclude it best to follow their exam-

ple in making use of the very same words with them both
in these articles (which are very many) wherein our faith and
doctrine are the same with theirs; and this we did the more
abundantly to manifest our consent with both in all the fundamental articles of the Christian religion, as also with many
others whose orthodox Confessions have been published to
the world on the behalf of the Protestants in diverse nations
and cities. And also to convince all that we have no itch to
clog religion with new words, but do readily acquiesce in that
form of sound words which hath been, in consent with the
Holy Scriptures, used by others before us; hereby declaring,
before God, angels, and men, our hearty agreement with
them in that wholesome Protestant doctrine which, with so
clear evidence of Scriptures, they have asserted. Some things,
indeed, are in some places added, some terms omitted, and
some few changed; but these alterations are of that nature as
that we need not doubt any charge or suspicion of unsound-
ness in the faith from any of our brethren upon the account
of them.

In those things wherein we differ from others we have
expressed ourselves with all candor and plainness, that none
might entertain jealousy of aught secretly lodged in our
breasts that we would not the world should be acquainted
with; yet we hope we have also observed those rules of mod-
esty and humility as will render our freedom in this respect
inoffensive, even to those whose sentiments are different
from ours.

We have also taken care to affix texts of Scripture at the
bottom, for the confirmation of each article in our Confes-

sion; in which work we have studiously endeavored to select such as are most clear and pertinent for the proof of what is asserted by us; and our earnest desire is that all into whose hands this may come would follow that (never enough commended) example of the noble Bereans, who searched the Scriptures daily that they might find out whether the things preached to them were so or not.

There is one thing more which we sincerely profess and earnestly desire credence in—viz., that contention is most remote from our design in all that we have done in this matter; and we hope that the liberty of an ingenuous unfolding our principles and opening our hearts unto our brethren, with the Scripture grounds of our faith and practice will by none of them be either denied to us, or taken ill from us. Our whole design is accomplished if we may have attained that justice as to be measured in our principles and practice, and the judgment of both by others, according to what we have now published, which the Lord (whose eyes are as a flame of fire) knoweth to be the doctrine which with our hearts we most firmly believe and sincerely endeavor to conform our lives to. And O that, other contentions being laid asleep, the only care and contention of all upon whom the name of our blessed Redeemer is called might for the future be to walk humbly with their God in the exercise of all love and meekness toward each other, to perfect holiness in the fear of the Lord, each one endeavoring to have his conversation such as becometh the Gospel; and also, suitable to his place and capacity, vigorously to promote in others the practice of true religion and undefiled in the sight of God our Father! And that in this backsliding day we might not spend our breath in fruitless complaints of the evils of others, but may every one begin at home, to reform in the first place our own hearts and ways, and then to quicken all that we may have influence upon to the same work, that if the will of God were so, none might deceive themselves by resting in and trusting to a form of godliness without the power of it, and inward experience of the efficacy of those truths that are professed by them.

And verily there is one spring and cause of the decay of religion in our day which we cannot but touch upon and earnestly urge a redress of, and that is the neglect of the worship of God in families by those to whom the charge and conduct of them is committed. May not the gross ignorance and instability of many, with the profaneness of others, be justly charged upon their parents and masters, who have not trained them up in the way wherein they ought to walk when they were young, but have neglected those frequent and solemn commands which the Lord hath laid upon them, so to catechize and instruct them that their tender years might be seasoned with the knowledge of the truth of God as revealed in the Scriptures; and also by their own omission of prayer and other duties of religion of their families, together with the ill example of their loose conversation, having, inured them first to a neglect and the contempt of all piety and religion? We know this will not excuse the blindness and wickedness of any, but certainly it will fall heavy upon those that have been thus the occasion thereof; they indeed die in their sins, but will not their blood be required of those under whose care they were, who yet permitted them to go on without warning—yea, led them into the paths of destruction? And will not the diligence of Christians with respect to the discharge of these duties in ages past rise up in judgment against and condemn many of those who would be esteemed such now?

We shall conclude with our earnest prayer that the God of all grace will pour out those measures of His Holy Spirit upon us, that the profession of truth may be accompanied with the sound belief and diligent practice of it by us, that His name may in all things be glorified through Jesus Christ our Lord. Amen.

All other thoughts on the matter of salvation / faith / obedience are useless, worthless. Scripture ALONE is the authority.

THE BAPTIST CONFESSION OF FAITH

CHAPTER 1
OF THE HOLY SCRIPTURES

Paragraph 1. The Holy Scripture is the (only) sufficient, certain, and infallible rule of all saving knowledge, faith, and obedience.[1] Although the light of nature, and the works of creation and providence do so far manifest the goodness, wisdom, and power of God, as to leave men inexcusable; yet they are not sufficient to give that knowledge of God and His will which is necessary unto salvation.[2] Therefore it pleased the Lord at sundry times and in divers manners to reveal Himself, and to declare that His will unto His church;[3] and afterward for the better preserving and propagating of the truth, and for the more sure establishment and comfort of the church against the corruption of the flesh, and the malice of Satan, and of the world, to commit the same wholly unto writing; which maketh the Holy Scriptures to be most necessary, those former ways of God's revealing His will unto His people being now ceased.[4]

[1] 2 Timothy 3:15-17; Isaiah 8:20; Luke 16:29,31; Ephesians 2:20
[2] Romans 1:19-21; 2:14,15; Psalm 19:1-3
[3] Hebrews 1:1
[4] Proverbs 22:19-21; Romans 15:4; 2 Peter 1:19,20

Paragraph 2. Under the name of Holy Scripture, or the Word of God written, are now contained all the books of the Old and New Testament, which are these:

OF THE OLD TESTAMENT:
Genesis, Exodus, Leviticus, Numbers, Deuteronomy, Joshua, Judges, Ruth, 1 Samuel, 2 Samuel, 1 Kings,

2 Kings, 1 Chronicles, 2 Chronicles, Ezra, Nehemiah, Esther, Job, Psalms, Proverbs, Ecclesiastes, The Song of Solomon, Isaiah, Jeremiah, Lamentations, Ezekiel, Daniel, Hosea, Joel, Amos, Obadiah, Jonah, Micah, Nahum, Habakkuk, Zephaniah, Haggai, Zechariah, Malachi.

OF THE NEW TESTAMENT:

Matthew, Mark, Luke, John, Acts, Romans, 1 Corinthians, 2 Corinthians, Galatians, Ephesians, Philippians, Colossians, 1 Thessalonians, 2 Thessalonians, 1 Timothy, 2 Timothy, Titus, Philemon, Hebrews, James, 1 Peter, 2 Peter, 1 John, 2 John, 3 John, Jude, Revelation.

All of which are given by the inspiration of God, to be the rule of faith and life.[5]

[5] 2 Timothy 3:16

Paragraph 3. The books commonly called Apocrypha, not being of divine inspiration, are no part of the canon or rule of the Scripture, and, therefore, are of no authority to the church of God, nor to be any otherwise approved or made use of than other human writings.[6]

[6] Luke 24:27,44; Romans 3:2

Paragraph 4. The authority of the Holy Scripture, for which it ought to be believed, dependeth not upon the testimony of any man or church, but wholly upon God (who is truth itself), the author thereof; therefore it is to be received because it is the Word of God.[7]

[7] 2 Peter 1:19-21; 2 Timothy 3:16; 1 Thessalonians 2:13; 1 John 5:9

Paragraph 5. We may be moved and induced by the testimony of the church of God to a high and reverent esteem of the Holy Scriptures; and the heavenliness of the matter, the efficacy of the doctrine, and the majesty of the style, the consent of all the parts, the scope of the whole (which is to give all glory to God), the full discovery it makes of the only way of man's salvation, and many other incomparable excellencies, and entire perfections thereof, are arguments whereby it doth abundantly evidence itself to be the Word of God; yet notwithstanding, our full persuasion and assurance of the infallible truth, and divine authority thereof, is from the inward work of the Holy Spirit bearing witness by and with the Word in our hearts.[8]

[8] John 16:13,14; 1 Corinthians 2:10-12; 1 John 2:20,27

Paragraph 6. The whole counsel of God concerning all things necessary for His own glory, man's salvation, faith and life, is either expressly set down or necessarily contained in the Holy Scripture: unto which nothing at any time is to be added, whether by new revelation of the Spirit, or traditions of men.[9]

Nevertheless, we acknowledge the inward illumination of the Spirit of God to be necessary for the saving understanding of such things as are revealed in the Word,[10] and that there are some circumstances concerning the worship of God, and government of the church, common to human actions and societies, which are to be ordered by the light of nature and Christian prudence, according to the general rules of the Word, which are always to be observed.[11]

[9] 2 Timothy 3:15-17; Galatians 1:8,9

[10] John 6:45; 1 Corinthians 2:9-12
[11] 1 Corinthians 11:13,14; 1 Corinthians 14:26,40

Paragraph 7. All things in Scripture are not alike plain in themselves, nor alike clear unto all;[12] yet those things which are necessary to be known, believed and observed for salvation, are so clearly propounded and opened in some place of Scripture or other, that not only the learned, but the unlearned, in a due use of ordinary means, may attain to a sufficient understanding of them.[13]

[12] 2 Peter 3:16
[13] Psalm 19:7; 119:130

Paragraph 8. The Old Testament in Hebrew (which was the native language of the people of God of old),[14] and the New Testament in Greek (which at the time of the writing of it was most generally known to the nations), being immediately inspired by God, and by His singular care and providence kept pure in all ages, are therefore authentic; so as in all controversies of religion, the church is finally to appeal to them.[15] But because these original tongues are not known to all the people of God, who have a right unto, and interest in the Scriptures, and are commanded in the fear of God to read,[16] and search them,[17] therefore they are to be translated into the vulgar language of every nation unto which they come,[18] that the Word of God dwelling plentifully in all, they may worship Him in an acceptable manner, and through patience and comfort of the Scriptures may have hope.[19]

[14] Romans 3:2
[15] Isaiah 8:20

[16] Acts 15:15
[17] John 5:39
[18] 1 Corinthians 14:6,9,11,12,24,28
[19] Colossians 3:16

Paragraph 9. The infallible rule of interpretation of Scripture is the Scripture itself; and therefore when there is a question about the true and full sense of any Scripture (which is not manifold, but one), it must be searched by other places that speak more clearly.[20]

[20] 2 Peter 1:20,21; Acts 15:15,16

Paragraph 10. The supreme judge, by which all controversies of religion are to be determined, and all decrees of councils, opinions of ancient writers, doctrines of men, and private spirits, are to be examined, and in whose sentence we are to rest, can be no other but the Holy Scripture delivered by the Spirit, into which Scripture so delivered, our faith is finally resolved.[21]

[21] Matthew 22:29,31; Ephesians 2:20; Acts 28:23

CHAPTER 2
OF GOD AND OF THE HOLY TRINITY

Paragraph 1. The Lord our God is but one only living and true God;[1] whose subsistence is in and of Himself,[2] infinite in being and perfection; whose essence cannot be comprehended by any but Himself;[3] a most pure spirit,[4] invisible, without body, parts, or passions, who only hath immortality, dwelling in the light which no man can approach unto;[5] who is immutable,[6] immense,[7] eternal,[8] incomprehensible, almighty,[9] every way infinite, most holy,[10] most wise, most free, most absolute; working all things according to the counsel of His own immutable and most righteous will,[11] for His own glory;[12] most loving, gracious, merciful, long-suffering, abundant in goodness and truth, forgiving iniquity, transgression, and sin; the rewarder of them that diligently seek Him,[13] and withal most just and terrible in His judgments,[14] hating all sin,[15] and who will by no means clear the guilty.[16]

[1] 1 Corinthians 8:4,6; Deuteronomy 6:4
[2] Jeremiah 10:10; Isaiah 48:12
[3] Exodus 3:14
[4] John 4:24
[5] 1 Timothy 1:17; Deuteronomy 4:15,16
[6] Malachi 3:6
[7] 1 Kings 8:27; Jeremiah 23:23
[8] Psalm 90:2
[9] Genesis 17:1
[10] Isaiah 6:3
[11] Psalm 115:3; Isaiah 46:10
[12] Proverbs 16:4; Romans 11:36
[13] Exodus 34:6,7; Hebrews 11:6
[14] Nehemiah 9:32,33
[15] Psalm 5:5,6
[16] Exodus 34:7; Nahum 1:2,3

Paragraph 2. God, having all life,[17] glory,[18] goodness,[19] blessedness, in and of Himself, is alone in and unto Himself all-sufficient, not standing in need of any creature which He hath made, nor deriving any glory from them,[20] but only manifesting His own glory in, by, unto, and upon them; He is the alone fountain of all being, of whom, through whom, and to whom are all things,[21] and He hath most sovereign dominion over all creatures, to do by them, for them, or upon them, whatsoever Himself pleaseth;[22] in His sight all things are open and manifest,[23] His knowledge is infinite, infallible, and independent upon the creature, so as nothing is to Him contingent or uncertain;[24] He is most holy in all His counsels, in all His works,[25] and in all His commands; to Him is due from angels and men, whatsoever worship,[26] service, or obedience, as creatures they owe unto the Creator, and whatever He is further pleased to require of them.

[17] John 5:26
[18] Psalm 148:13
[19] Psalm 119:68
[20] Job 22:2,3
[21] Romans 11:34-36
[22] Daniel 4:25,34,35
[23] Hebrews 4:13
[24] Ezekiel 11:5; Acts 15:18
[25] Psalm 145:17
[26] Revelation 5:12-14

Paragraph 3. In this divine and infinite Being there are three subsistences, the Father, the Word (or Son), and Holy Spirit,[27] of one substance, power, and eternity, each having the whole divine essence, yet the essence undivided:[28] the Father is of none, neither begotten nor proceeding; the Son is eternally begotten of the Father;[29] the Holy Spirit proceeding from the Father and the Son;[30] all infinite, without beginning, therefore but one God, who is not to be divided in nature and being, but distinguished by several peculiar relative properties

and personal relations; which doctrine of the Trinity is the
foundation of all our communion with God, and comfortable
dependence on Him.

[27] 1 John 5:7; Matthew 28:19; 2 Corinthians 13:14
[28] Exodus 3:14; John 14:11; 1 Corinthians 8:6
[29] John 1:14,18
[30] John 15:26; Galatians 4:6

CHAPTER 3
OF GOD'S DECREE

Paragraph 1. God hath decreed in Himself, from all eternity,
by the most wise and holy counsel of His own will freely
and unchangeably, all things, whatsoever comes to pass;[1] yet
so as thereby is God neither the author of sin nor hath fellowship with any therein;[2] nor is violence offered to the will
of the creature, nor yet is the liberty or contingency of second
causes taken away, but rather established;[3] in which appears
His wisdom in disposing all things, and power and faithfulness
in accomplishing His decree.[4]

[1] Isaiah 46:10; Ephesians 1:11; Hebrews 6:17; Romans 9:15,18
[2] James 1:13; 1 John 1:5
[3] Acts 4:27,28; John 19:11
[4] Numbers 23:19; Ephesians 1:3-5

Paragraph 2. Although God knoweth whatsoever may or can
come to pass, upon all supposed conditions,[5] yet hath He not
decreed anything, because He foresaw it as future, or as that
which would come to pass upon such conditions.[6]

[5] Acts 15:18
[6] Romans 9:11,13,16,18

God did not "look through the corridors of time." He has foreordained everything.

Paragraph 3. By the decree of God, for the (manifestation) of His (glory,) some men and angels are predestinated, or foreordained to eternal life through Jesus Christ,[7] to the praise of His glorious grace;[8] others being left to act in their sin to their just condemnation, to the praise of His glorious (justice.[9])

[7] 1 Timothy 5:21; Matthew 25:34
[8] Ephesians 1:5,6
[9] Romans 9:22,23; Jude 4

Paragraph 4. These angels and men thus predestinated and foreordained, are particularly and unchangeably designed, and their number so (certain) and (definite) that it cannot be either increased or diminished.[10]

[10] 2 Timothy 2:19; John 13:18

Paragraph 5. Those of mankind that are predestinated to life, God, before the foundation of the world was laid, according to His eternal and immutable purpose, and the (secret) counsel and good pleasure of His will, hath chosen in Christ unto everlasting glory, out of His mere free grace and love,[11] without any other thing in the creature as a condition or cause moving Him thereunto.[12]

I cannot save myself OR sustain my salvation!

[11] Ephesians 1:4,9,11; Romans 8:30; 2 Timothy 1:9;
      1 Thessalonians 5:9
[12] Romans 9:13,16; Ephesians 2:5,12

Paragraph 6. As God hath appointed the elect unto glory, so He hath, by the eternal and most free purpose of His will, foreordained all the means thereunto;[13] wherefore they who are elected, being fallen in Adam, are redeemed by Christ,[14] are effectually called unto faith in Christ, by His Spirit working in due season, are justified, adopted, sanctified,[15] and kept by His power through faith unto salvation;[16] neither are any other redeemed by Christ, or effectually called, justified, adopted, sanctified, and saved, but the elect only.[17]

[13] 1 Peter 1:2; 2 Thessalonians 2:13
[14] 1 Thessalonians 5:9,10
[15] Romans 8:30; 2 Thessalonians 2:13
[16] 1 Peter 1:5
[17] John 10:26, 17:9, 6:64

Paragraph 7. The doctrine of this high mystery of predestination is to be handled with special prudence and care, that men attending the will of God revealed in His Word, and yielding obedience thereunto, may, from the certainty of their effectual vocation, be assured of their eternal election;[18] so shall this doctrine afford matter of praise,[19] reverence, and admiration of God, and of humility,[20] diligence, and abundant consolation to all that sincerely obey the Gospel.[21]

[18] 1 Thessalonians 1:4,5; 2 Peter 1:10
[19] Ephesians 1:6; Romans 11:33
[20] Romans 11:5,6,20
[21] Luke 10:20

CHAPTER 4
OF CREATION

Made from Him, through Him, and to Him - His glory is the purpose.

Paragraph 1. In the beginning it pleased God the Father, Son, and Holy Spirit,[1] for the manifestation of the glory of His eternal power,[2] wisdom, and goodness, to create or make the world, and all things therein, whether visible or invisible, in the space of six days, and all very good.[3]

[1] John 1:2,3; Hebrews 1:2; Job 26:13
[2] Romans 1:20
[3] Colossians 1:16; Genesis 1:31

They were ABLE to obey completely! They chose not to. As unbelievers, until God puts life in our hearts, we are only free to

Paragraph 2. After God had made all other creatures, He created man, male and female,[4] with reasonable and immortal souls,[5] rendering them fit unto that life to God for which they were created; being made after the image of God, in knowledge, righteousness, and true holiness;[6] having the law of God written in their hearts,[7] and power to fulfill it, and yet under a possibility of transgressing, being left to the liberty of their own will, which was subject to change.[8]

disobey and we continually freely choose to. We cannot obey until He saves us

[4] Genesis 1:27
[5] Genesis 2:7
[6] Ecclesiastes 7:29; Genesis 1:26
[7] Romans 2:14,15
[8] Genesis 3:6

*"free will" - free to obey
for - free to sin
Adam + - commanded to obey
Eve - commanded not to sin
Unsaved - free will used for sin only
us:
Saved us: free will restored so we can choose obedience to all His Command*

Paragraph 3. Besides the law written in their hearts, they received a command not to eat of the tree of knowledge of good and evil,[9] which while they kept, they were happy in their communion with God, and had dominion over the creatures.[10]

[9] Genesis 2:17
[10] Genesis 1:26,28

CHAPTER 5
OF DIVINE PROVIDENCE

Paragraph 1. God the good Creator of all things, in His infinite power and wisdom doth uphold, direct, dispose, and govern all creatures and things,[1] from the greatest even to the least,[2] by His most wise and holy providence, to the end for the which they were created, according unto His infallible foreknowledge, and the free and immutable counsel of His own will; to the praise of the glory of His wisdom, power, justice, infinite goodness, and mercy.[3]

[1] Hebrews 1:3; Job 38:11; Isaiah 46:10,11; Psalm 135:6
[2] Matthew 10:29-31
[3] Ephesians 1:11

Paragraph 2. Although in relation to the foreknowledge and decree of God, the first cause, all things come to pass immutably and infallibly;[4] so that there is not anything befalls any by chance, or without His providence;[5] yet by the same providence He ordereth them to fall out according to the nature of second causes, either necessarily, freely, or contingently.[6]

[4] Acts 2:23
[5] Proverbs 16:33
[6] Genesis 8:22

Paragraph 3. God, in His ordinary providence maketh use of means,[7] yet is free to work without,[8] above,[9] and against them[10] at His pleasure.

[7] Acts 27:31,44; Isaiah 55:10,11
[8] Hosea 1:7

[9] Romans 4:19-21
[10] Daniel 3:27

Paragraph 4. The almighty power, unsearchable wisdom, and infinite goodness of God, so far manifest themselves in His providence, that His determinate counsel extendeth itself even to the first fall, and all other sinful actions both of angels and men;[11] and that not by a bare permission, which also He most wisely and powerfully boundeth, and otherwise ordereth and governeth,[12] in a manifold dispensation to His most holy ends;[13] yet so, as the sinfulness of their acts proceedeth only from the creatures, and not from God, who, being most holy and righteous, neither is nor can be the author or approver of sin.[14]

[11] Romans 11:32-34; 2 Samuel 24:1; 1 Chronicles 21:1
[12] 2 Kings 19:28; Psalm 76:10
[13] Genesis 50:20; Isaiah 10:6,7,12
[14] Psalm 50:21; 1 John 2:16

Paragraph 5. The most wise, righteous, and gracious God doth oftentimes leave for a season His own children to manifold temptations and the corruptions of their own hearts, to chastise them for their former sins, or to discover unto them the hidden strength of corruption and deceitfulness of their hearts, that they may be humbled; and to raise them to a more close and constant dependence for their support upon Himself; and to make them more watchful against all future occasions of sin, and for other just and holy ends.[15] So that whatsoever befalls any of His elect is by His appointment, for His glory, and their good.[16]

"I feel far from God"
– then remember there is a good reason. Either you ran or

He is teaching you something for His glory + your good.

[15] 2 Chronicles 32:25,26,31; 2 Corinthians 12:7-9
[16] Romans 8:28

Paragraph 6. As for those wicked and ungodly men whom God, as the righteous judge, for former sin doth blind and harden;[17] from them He not only withholdeth His grace, whereby they might have been enlightened in their understanding, and wrought upon their hearts;[18] but sometimes also withdraweth the gifts which they had,[19] and exposeth them to such objects as their corruption makes occasion of sin;[20] and withal, gives them over to their own lusts, the temptations of the world, and the power of Satan,[21] whereby it comes to pass that they harden themselves even under those means which God useth for the softening of others.[22]

(margin note: All for His own glory. He is holy and all He does is just and good.)

[17] Romans 1:24-26,28, 11:7,8
[18] Deuteronomy 29:4
[19] Matthew 13:12
[20] Deuteronomy 2:30; 2 Kings 8:12,13
[21] Psalm 81:11,12; 2 Thessalonians 2:10-12
[22] Exodus 8:15,32; Isaiah 6:9,10; 1 Peter 2:7,8

(margin note: This truth ought to sober me to "live worthy" because Jesus made me worthy. I am no different from the wicked apart from His grace.)

(note: Romans 9 - the Potter has a right to do what He will with His clay.)

Paragraph 7. As the providence of God doth in general reach to all creatures, so after a most special manner it taketh care of His church, and disposeth of all things to the good thereof.[23]

[23] 1 Timothy 4:10; Amos 9:8,9; Isaiah 43:3-5

CHAPTER 6

OF THE FALL OF MAN, OF SIN, AND OF THE PUNISHMENT THEREOF

Paragraph 1. Although God created man upright and perfect, and gave him a righteous law, which had been unto life had he kept it, and threatened death upon the breach thereof,[1] yet he did not long abide in this honor; Satan using the subtlety of the serpent to seduce Eve, then by her seducing Adam, who, without any compulsion, did willfully transgress the law of their creation, and the command given unto them, in eating the forbidden fruit,[2] which God was pleased, according to His wise and holy counsel to permit, having purposed to order it to His own glory.

[1] Genesis 2:16,17
[2] Genesis 3:12,13; 2 Corinthians 11:3

Paragraph 2. Our first parents, by this sin, fell from their original righteousness and communion with God, and we in them whereby death came upon all:[3] all becoming dead in sin,[4] and wholly defiled in all the faculties and parts of soul and body.[5]

[3] Romans 3:23
[4] Romans 5:12
[5] Titus 1:15; Genesis 6:5; Jeremiah 17:9; Romans 3:10-19

Paragraph 3. They being the root, and by God's appointment, standing in the room and stead of all mankind, the guilt of the sin was imputed, and corrupted nature conveyed, to all their posterity descending from them by ordinary generation,[6] being now conceived in sin,[7] and by nature children of wrath,[8] the servants of sin, the subjects of death,[9] and all other miseries, spiritual, temporal, and eternal, unless the Lord Jesus set them free.[10]

[6] Romans 5:12-19; 1 Corinthians 15:21,22,45,49
[7] Psalm 51:5; Job 14:4
[8] Ephesians 2:3
[9] Romans 6:20, 5:12
[10] Hebrews 2:14,15; 1 Thessalonians 1:10

Paragraph 4. From this original corruption, whereby we are utterly indisposed, disabled, and made opposite to all good, and wholly inclined to all evil,[11] do proceed all actual transgressions.[12]

[11] Romans 8:7; Colossians 1:21
[12] James 1:14,15; Matthew 15:19

Paragraph 5. The corruption of nature, during this life, does remain in those that are regenerated;[13] and although it be through Christ pardoned and mortified, yet both itself, and the first motions thereof, are truly and properly sin.[14]

[13] Romans 7:18,23; Ecclesiastes 7:20; 1 John 1:8
[14] Romans 7:23-25; Galatians 5:17

CHAPTER 7
OF GOD'S COVENANT

Paragraph 1. The distance between God and the creature is so great, that although reasonable creatures do owe obedience to Him as their creator, yet they could never have attained the reward of life but by some voluntary condescension on God's part, which He hath been pleased to express by way of covenant.[1]

[1] Luke 17:10; Job 35:7,8

Paragraph 2. Moreover, man having brought himself under the curse of the law by his fall, it pleased the Lord to make a covenant of grace,[2] wherein He freely offers unto sinners life and salvation by Jesus Christ, requiring of them faith in Him, that they may be saved;[3] and promising to give unto all those that are ordained unto eternal life, His Holy Spirit, to make them willing and able to believe.[4]

[2] Genesis 2:17; Galatians 3:10; Romans 3:20,21
[3] Romans 8:3; Mark 16:15,16; John 3:16;
[4] Ezekiel 36:26,27; John 6:44,45; Psalm 110:3

Paragraph 3. This covenant is revealed in the gospel; first of all to Adam in the promise of salvation by the seed of the woman,[5] and afterwards by farther steps, until the full discovery thereof was completed in the New Testament;[6] and it is founded in that eternal covenant transaction that was between the Father and the Son about the redemption of the elect;[7] and it is alone by the grace of this covenant that all the posterity of fallen Adam that ever were saved did obtain life and blessed immortality, man being now utterly incapable of acceptance with God upon those terms on which Adam stood in his state of innocency.[8]

[5] Genesis 3:15
[6] Hebrews 1:1
[7] 2 Timothy 1:9; Titus 1:2
[8] Hebrews 11:6,13; Romans 4:1,2; Acts 4:12; John 8:56

CHAPTER 8
OF CHRIST THE MEDIATOR

Paragraph 1. <u>It pleased God,</u> in His eternal purpose, to choose and ordain the Lord Jesus, His only begotten Son, according to the covenant made between them both, to be the mediator between God and man;[1] the prophet,[2] priest,[3] and king;[4] Head and Savior of His Church,[5] the heir of all things,[6] and judge of the world;[7] unto whom He did from all eternity give a people to be His seed and to be by Him in time redeemed, called, justified, sanctified, and glorified.[8]

[1] Isaiah 42:1; 1 Peter 1:19,20
[2] Acts 3:22
[3] Hebrews 5:5,6
[4] Psalm 2:6; Luke 1:33
[5] Ephesians 1:22,23
[6] Hebrews 1:2
[7] Acts 17:31
[8] Isaiah 53:10; John 17:6; Romans 8:30

Paragraph 2. The Son of God, the second person in the Holy Trinity, being very and eternal God, the brightness of the Father's glory, of one substance and equal with Him, who made the world, who upholds and governs all things He has made, did, when the fullness of time was come, take upon Him man's nature, with all the essential properties and common infirmities thereof,[9] yet without sin;[10] being conceived by the Holy Spirit in the womb of the Virgin Mary, the Holy Spirit coming down upon her, and the power of the Most High overshadowing her, and so was made of a woman, of the tribe of Judah, of the seed of Abraham and David, according to the Scriptures;[11] so that two whole, perfect, and distinct natures were inseparably joined together in one person, without conversion, composition, or confusion; which person is very God and very man, yet one Christ, the only mediator between God and man.[12]

[9] John 1:14; Galatians 4:4
[10] Romans 8:3; Hebrews 2:14,16,17, 4:15
[11] Matthew 1:22,23; Luke 1:27,31,35
[12] Romans 9:5; 1 Timothy 2:5

Paragraph 3. The Lord Jesus, in His human nature thus united to the divine, in the person of the Son, was sanctified and anointed with the Holy Spirit above measure,[13] having in Him all the treasures of wisdom and knowledge;[14] in whom it pleased the Father that all fullness should dwell,[15] to the end that being holy, harmless, undefiled,[16] and full of grace and truth,[17] He might be throughly furnished to execute the office of mediator and surety;[18] which office He took not upon Himself, but was thereunto called by His Father;[19] who also put all power and judgment in His hand, and gave Him commandment to execute the same.[20]

[13] Psalm 45:7; Acts 10:38; John 3:34
[14] Colossians 2:3
[15] Colossians 1:19
[16] Hebrews 7:26
[17] John 1:14
[18] Hebrews 7:22
[19] Hebrews 5:5
[20] John 5:22,27; Matthew 28:18; Acts 2:36

Paragraph 4. This office the Lord Jesus did most willingly undertake,[21] which that He might discharge He was made under the law,[22] and did perfectly fulfill it, and underwent the punishment due to us, which we should have born and suffered,[23] being made sin and a curse for us;[24] enduring most grievous sorrows in His soul, and most painful sufferings in His body;[25] was crucified, and died, and remained in the state of the dead, yet saw no corruption:[26] on the third day He arose from the dead[27] with the same body in which He suffered,[28] with which He also ascended into heaven,[29] and there sits at the right hand of His Father, making intercession,[30] and shall return to judge men and angels at the end of the world.[31]

[21] Psalm 40:7,8; Hebrews 10:5-10; John 10:18
[22] Galatians 4:4; Matthew 3:15
[23] Galatians 3:13; Isaiah 53:6; 1 Peter 3:18
[24] 2 Corinthians 5:21
[25] Matthew 26:37,38; Luke 22:44; Matthew 27:46
[26] Acts 13:37
[27] 1 Corinthians 15:3,4
[28] John 20:25,27
[29] Mark 16:19; Acts 1:9-11
[30] Romans 8:34; Hebrews 9:24
[31] Acts 10:42; Romans 14:9,10; Acts 1:11; 2 Peter 2:4

Paragraph 5. The Lord Jesus, by His perfect obedience and sacrifice of Himself, which He through the eternal Spirit once offered up to God, has fully satisfied the justice of God,[32] procured reconciliation, and purchased an everlasting inheritance in the kingdom of heaven for all those whom the Father has given unto Him.[33]

[32] Hebrews 9:14, 10:14; Romans 3:25,26
[33] John 17:2; Hebrews 9:15

Paragraph 6. Although the price of redemption was not actually paid by Christ until after His incarnation, yet the virtue, efficacy, and benefit thereof were communicated to the elect in all ages successively from the beginning of the world, in and by those promises, types, and sacrifices wherein He was revealed, and signified to be the seed of the woman which should bruise the serpent's head;[34] and the Lamb slain from the foundation of the world,[35] being the same yesterday, and today and for ever.[36]

[34] 1 Corinthians 4:10; Hebrews 4:2; 1 Peter 1:10,11
[35] Revelation 13:8
[36] Hebrews 13:8

Paragraph 7. Christ, in the work of mediation, acts according to both natures, by each nature doing that which is proper to itself; yet by reason of the unity of the person, that which is proper to one nature is sometimes in Scripture, attributed to the person denominated by the other nature.[37]

[37] John 3:13; Acts 20:28

Paragraph 8. To all those for whom Christ has obtained eternal redemption, He does certainly and effectually apply and communicate the same, making intercession for them;[38] uniting them to Himself by His Spirit, revealing to them, in and by the Word, the mystery of salvation, persuading them to believe and obey,[39] governing their hearts by His Word and Spirit,[40] and overcoming all their enemies by His almighty power and wisdom,[41] in such manner and ways as are most consonant to His wonderful and unsearchable dispensation; and all of free and absolute grace, without any condition foreseen in them to procure it.[42]

[38] John 6:37, 10:15,16, 17:9; Romans 5:10
[39] John 17:6; Ephesians 1:9; 1 John 5:20
[40] Romans 8:9,14
[41] Psalm 110:1; 1 Corinthians 15:25,26
[42] John 3:8; Ephesians 1:8

Paragraph 9. This office of mediator between God and man is proper only to Christ, who is the prophet, priest, and king of the church of God; and may not be either in whole, or any part thereof, transferred from Him to any other.[43]

[43] 1 Timothy 2:5

Paragraph 10. This number and order of offices is necessary; for in respect of our ignorance, we stand in need of His prophetical office;[44] and in respect of our alienation from God, and imperfection of the best of our services, we need His priestly office to reconcile us and present us acceptable unto God;[45] and in respect of our averseness and utter inability to return to God, and for our rescue and security from our spiritual adversaries, we need His kingly office to convince, subdue, draw, uphold, deliver, and preserve us to His heavenly kingdom.[46]

[44] John 1:18
[45] Colossians 1:21; Galatians 5:17
[46] John 16:8; Psalm 110:3; Luke 1:74,75

CHAPTER 9
OF FREE WILL

Paragraph 1. God has endued the will of man with that natural liberty and power of acting upon choice, that it is neither forced, nor by any necessity of nature determined to do good or evil.[1]

[1] Matthew 17:12; James 1:14; Deuteronomy 30:19

Paragraph 2. Man, in his state of innocency, had freedom and power to will and to do that which was good and well-pleasing to God,[2] but yet was mutable so that he might fall from it.[3]

[2] Ecclesiastes 7:29
[3] Genesis 3:6

Paragraph 3. Man, by his fall into a state of sin, has wholly lost all ability of will to any spiritual good accompanying salvation;[4] so as a natural man, being altogether averse from that good, and dead in sin,[5] is not able by his own strength to convert himself, or to prepare himself thereunto.[6]

[4] Romans 5:6, 8:7
[5] Ephesians 2:1,5
[6] Titus 3:3-5; John 6:44

Paragraph 4. When God converts a sinner, and translates him into the state of grace, He frees him from his natural bondage under sin,[7] and by His grace alone enables him freely to will and to do that which is spiritually good;[8] yet so as that by reason of his remaining corruptions, he does not perfectly,

nor only will that which is good, but does also will that which
is evil.[9]

[7] Colossians 1:13; John 8:36
[8] Philippians 2:13
[9] Romans 7:15,18,19,21,23

Paragraph 5. This will of man is made perfectly and immutably
free to good alone in the state of glory only.[10]

[10] Ephesians 4:13

CHAPTER 10
OF EFFECTUAL CALLING

Paragraph 1. Those whom God hath predestinated unto life,
He is pleased in His appointed and accepted time, effectually to call,[1] by His Word and Spirit, out of that state of sin
and death in which they are by nature, to grace and salvation
by Jesus Christ;[2] enlightening their minds spiritually and sav-
ingly to understand the things of God;[3] taking away their
heart of stone; and giving to them a heart of flesh;[4] renewing their wills, and by His almighty power determining them
to that which is good, and effectually drawing them to Jesus
Christ;[5] yet so as they come most freely, being made willing
by His grace.[6]

[1] Romans 8:30, 11:7; Ephesians 1:10,11; 2 Thessalonians 2:13,14
[2] Ephesians 2:1-6
[3] Acts 26:18; Ephesians 1:17,18
[4] Ezekiel 36:26
[5] Deuteronomy 30:6; Ezekiel 36:27; Ephesians 1:19
[6] Psalm 110:3; Song of Solomon 1:4

Paragraph 2. This effectual call is of God's free and special grace alone, not from anything at all foreseen in man, nor from any power or agency in the creature co-working with His Special grace,[7] the creature being wholly passive therein, being dead in sins and trespasses, until being quickened and renewed by the Holy Spirit;[8] he is thereby enabled to answer this call, and to embrace the grace offered and conveyed in it, and that by no less power than that which raised up Christ from the dead.[9]

[7] 2 Timothy 1:9; Ephesians 2:8
[8] 1 Corinthians 2:14; Ephesians 2:5; John 5:25
[9] Ephesians 1:19,20

Paragraph 3. Elect infants dying in infancy are regenerated and saved by Christ through the Spirit;[10] who works when, and where, and how He pleases;[11] so also are all other elect persons, who are incapable of being outwardly called by the ministry of the Word.

[10] John 3:3,5,6
[11] John 3:8

Paragraph 4. Others not elected, although they may be called by the ministry of the Word, and may have some common operations of the Spirit,[12] yet not being effectually drawn by the Father, they neither will nor can truly come to Christ, and therefore cannot be saved,[13] much less can men that do not receive the Christian religion be saved: be they never so diligent to frame their lives according to the light of nature and the law of that religion they do profess.[14]

[12] Matthew 22:14, 13:20,21; Hebrews 6:4,5
[13] John 6:44,45,65; 1 John 2:24,25
[14] Acts 4:12; John 4:22, 17:3

CHAPTER 11
OF JUSTIFICATION

Paragraph 1. Those whom God effectually calls, he also freely justifies,[1] not by infusing righteousness into them, but by pardoning their sins, and by accounting and accepting their persons as righteous;[2] not for anything wrought in them, or done by them, but for Christ's sake alone;[3] not by imputing faith itself, the act of believing, or any other evangelical obedience to them, as their righteousness; but by imputing Christ's active obedience unto the whole law, and passive obedience in his death for their whole and sole righteousness,[4] they receiving and resting on Him and His righteousness by faith, which faith they have not of themselves; it is the gift of God.[5]

[1] Romans 3:24, 8:30
[2] Romans 4:5-8, Ephesians 1:7
[3] 1 Corinthians 1:30,31, Romans 5:17-19
[4] Philippians 3:8,9; Ephesians 2:8-10
[5] John 1:12, Romans 5:17

Paragraph 2. Faith thus receiving and resting on Christ and His righteousness, is the alone instrument of justification;[6] yet is not alone in the person justified, but is ever accompanied with all other saving graces, and is no dead faith, but works by love.[7]

[6] Romans 3:28
[7] Galatians 5:6, James 2:17,22,26

Paragraph 3. Christ, by His obedience and death, did fully discharge the debt of all those who are justified; and did, by the sacrifice of Himself in the blood of His cross, undergoing in their stead the penalty due to them, make a proper, real, and full satisfaction to God's justice in their behalf;[8] yet, in as much as He was given by the Father for them, and His obedience and satisfaction accepted in their stead, and both freely, not for anything in them,[9] their justification is only of free grace, that both the exact justice and rich grace of God might be glorified in the justification of sinners.[10]

[8] Hebrews 10:14; 1 Peter 1:18,19; Isaiah 53:5,6
[9] Romans 8:32; 2 Corinthians 5:21
[10] Romans 3:26; Ephesians 1:6,7; 2:7

Paragraph 4. God did from all eternity decree to justify all the elect,[11] and Christ did in the fullness of time die for their sins, and rise again for their justification;[12] nevertheless, they are not justified personally, until the Holy Spirit does in due time actually apply Christ to them.[13]

[11] Galatians 3:8; 1 Peter 1:2; 1 Timothy 2:6
[12] Romans 4:25
[13] Colossians 1:21,22; Titus 3:4-7

Paragraph 5. God continues to forgive the sins of those that are justified,[14] and although they can never fall from the state of justification,[15] yet they may, by their sins, fall under God's fatherly displeasure;[16] and in that condition they usually do not have the light of His countenance restored to them, until they humble themselves, confess their sins, beg pardon, and renew their faith and repentance.[17]

[14] Matthew 6:12; 1 John 1:7,9
[15] John 10:28

[16] Psalm 89:31-33

[17] Psalm 32:5; Psalm 51; Matthew 26:75

Paragraph 6. The justification of believers under the Old Testament was, in all these respects, one and the same with the justification of believers under the New Testament.[18]

[18] Galatians 3:9; Romans 4:22-24

CHAPTER 12
OF ADOPTION

Paragraph 1. All those that are justified, God vouchsafed, in and for the sake of His only Son Jesus Christ, to make partakers of the grace of adoption,[1] by which they are taken into the number, and enjoy the liberties and privileges of the children of God,[2] have His name put on them,[3] receive the spirit of adoption,[4] have access to the throne of grace with boldness, are enabled to cry Abba, Father,[5] are pitied,[6] protected,[7] provided for,[8] and chastened by Him as by a Father,[9] yet never cast off,[10] but sealed to the day of redemption,[11] and inherit the promises as heirs of everlasting salvation.[12]

[1] Ephesians 1:5; Galatians 4:4,5

[2] John 1:12; Romans 8:17

[3] 2 Corinthians 6:18; Revelation 3:12

[4] Romans 8:15

[5] Galatians 4:6; Ephesians 2:18

[6] Psalm 103:13

[7] Proverbs 14:26

[8] 1 Peter 5:7

[9] Hebrews 12:6

[10] Isaiah 54:8,9; Lamentations 3:31
[11] Ephesians 4:30
[12] Hebrews 1:14; 6:12

CHAPTER 13
OF SANCTIFICATION

Paragraph 1. They who are united to Christ, effectually called, and regenerated, having a new heart and a new spirit created in them through the virtue of Christ's death and resurrection, are also farther sanctified, really and personally,[1] through the same virtue, by His Word and Spirit dwelling in them;[2] the dominion of the whole body of sin is destroyed,[3] and the several lusts thereof are more and more weakened and morti-fied,[4] and they more and more quickened and strengthened in all saving graces,[5] to the practice of all true holiness, without which no man shall see the Lord.[6]

[1] Acts 20:32; Romans 6:5,6
[2] John 17:17; Ephesians 3:16-19; 1 Thessalonians 5:21-23
[3] Romans 6:14
[4] Galatians 5:24
[5] Colossians 1:11
[6] 2 Corinthians 7:1; Hebrews 12:14

Paragraph 2. This sanctification is throughout, in the whole man,[7] yet imperfect in this life; there abideth still some rem-nants of corruption in every part,[8] whence ariseth a continual and irreconcilable war; the flesh lusting against the Spirit, and the Spirit against the flesh.[9]

[7] 1 Thessalonians 5:23

[8] Romans 7:18,23
[9] Galatians 5:17; 1 Peter 2:11

Paragraph 3. In which war, although the remaining corruption for a time may much prevail,[10] yet, through the continual supply of strength from the sanctifying Spirit of Christ, the regenerate part doth overcome;[11] and so the saints grow in grace, perfecting holiness in the fear of God, pressing after an heavenly life, in evangelical obedience to all the commands which Christ, as Head and King, in His Word hath prescribed to them.[12]

[10] Romans 7:23
[11] Romans 6:14
[12] Ephesians 4:15,16; 2 Corinthians 3:18; 7:1

CHAPTER 14
OF SAVING FAITH

Paragraph 1. The grace of faith, whereby the elect are enabled to believe to the saving of their souls, is the work of the Spirit of Christ in their hearts,[1] and is ordinarily wrought by the ministry of the Word;[2] by which also, and by the administration of baptism and the Lord's supper, prayer, and other means appointed of God, it is increased and strengthened.[3]

[1] 2 Corinthians 4:13; Ephesians 2:8
[2] Romans 10:14,17
[3] Luke 17:5; 1 Peter 2:2; Acts 20:32

Paragraph 2. By this faith a Christian believeth to be true whatsoever is revealed in the Word for the authority of God

Himself,[4] and also apprehendeth an excellency therein above all other writings and all things in the world,[5] as it bears forth the glory of God in His attributes, the excellency of Christ in His nature and offices, and the power and fullness of the Holy Spirit in His workings and operations: and so is enabled to cast his soul upon the truth thus believed;[6] and also acteth differently upon that which each particular passage thereof containeth; yielding obedience to the commands,[7] trembling at the threatenings,[8] and embracing the promises of God for this life and that which is to come;[9] but the principle acts of saving faith have immediate relation to Christ, accepting, receiving, and resting upon Him alone for justification, sanctification, and eternal life, by virtue of the covenant of grace.[10]

[4] Acts 24:14
[5] Psalm 19:7-10; 119:72
[6] 2 Timothy 1:12
[7] John 15:14
[8] Isaiah 66:2
[9] Hebrews 11:13
[10] John 1:12; Acts 16:31; Galatians 2:20; Acts 15:11

Paragraph 3. This faith, although it be different in degrees, and may be weak or strong,[11] yet it is in the least degree of it different in the kind or nature of it, as is all other saving grace, from the faith and common grace of temporary believers;[12] and therefore, though it may be many times assailed and weakened, yet it gets the victory,[13] growing up in many to the attainment of a full assurance through Christ,[14] who is both the author and finisher of our faith.[15]

[11] Hebrews 5:13,14; Matthew 6:30; Romans 4:19,20

[12] 2 Peter 1:1
[13] Ephesians 6:16; 1 John 5:4,5
[14] Hebrews 6:11,12; Colossians 2:2
[15] Hebrews 12:2

CHAPTER 15
OF REPENTANCE UNTO LIFE AND SALVATION

Paragraph 1. Such of the elect that are converted at riper years, having sometime lived in the state of nature, and therein served divers lusts and pleasures, God in their effectual calling giveth them repentance unto life.[1]

[1] Titus 3:2-5

Paragraph 2. Whereas there is none that doth good and sinneth not,[2] and the best of men may, through the power and deceitfulness of their corruption dwelling in them, with the prevalency of temptation, fall into great sins and provocations; God hath, in the covenant of grace, mercifully provided that believers so sinning and falling be renewed through repentance unto salvation.[3]

[2] Ecclesiastes 7:20
[3] Luke 22:31,32

Paragraph 3. This saving repentance is an evangelical grace,[4] whereby a person, being by the Holy Spirit made sensible of the manifold evils of his sin, doth, by faith in Christ, humble himself for it with godly sorrow, detestation of it, and selfabhorrency,[5] praying for pardon and strength of grace, with a purpose and endeavor, by supplies of the Spirit, to walk before God unto all well-pleasing in all things.[6]

[4] Zechariah 12:10; Acts 11:18
[5] Ezekiel 36:31; 2 Corinthians 7:11
[6] Psalm 119:6,128

Paragraph 4. As repentance is to be continued through the whole course of our lives, upon the account of the body of death, and the motions thereof, so it is every man's duty to repent of his particular known sins particularly.[7]

[7] Luke 19:8; 1 Timothy 1:13,15

Paragraph 5. Such is the provision which God hath made through Christ in the covenant of grace for the preservation of believers unto salvation, that although there is no sin so small but it deserves damnation,[8] yet there is no sin so great that it shall bring damnation on them that repent,[9] which makes the constant preaching of repentance necessary.

[8] Romans 6:23
[9] Isaiah 1:16-18; 55:7

CHAPTER 16
OF GOOD WORKS

Paragraph 1. Good works are only such as God hath commanded in His Holy Word,[1] and not such as without the warrant thereof are devised by men out of blind zeal, or upon any pretense of good intentions.[2]

[1] Micah 6:8; Hebrews 13:21
[2] Matthew 15:9; Isaiah 29:13

Paragraph 2. These good works, done in obedience to God's commandments, are the fruits and evidences of a true and lively faith;[3] and by them believers manifest their thankfulness,[4] strengthen their assurance,[5] edify their brethren, adorn the profession of the Gospel,[6] stop the mouths of the adversaries, and glorify God,[7] whose workmanship they are, created in Christ Jesus thereunto,[8] that having their fruit unto holiness they may have the end eternal life.[9]

[3] James 2:18,22
[4] Psalm 116:12,13
[5] 1 John 2:3,5; 2 Peter 1:5-11
[6] Matthew 5:16
[7] 1 Timothy 6:1; 1 Peter 2:15; Philippians 1:11
[8] Ephesians 2:10
[9] Romans 6:22

Paragraph 3. Their ability to do good works is not at all of themselves, but wholly from the Spirit of Christ;[10] and that they may be enabled thereunto, besides the graces they have already received, there is necessary an actual influence of the same Holy Spirit, to work in them to will and to do of His good pleasure;[11] yet they are not hereupon to grow negligent, as if they were not bound to perform any duty, unless upon a special motion of the Spirit, but they ought to be diligent in stirring up the grace of God that is in them.[12]

[10] John 15:4,5
[11] 2 Corinthians 3:5; Philippians 2:13
[12] Philippians 2:12; Hebrews 6:11,12; Isaiah 64:7

Paragraph 4. They who in their obedience attain to the greatest height which is possible in this life, are so far from being able to supererogate, and to do more than God requires, as that they fall short of much which in duty they are bound to do.[13]

[13] Job 9:2, 3; Galatians 5:17; Luke 17:10

Paragraph 5. We cannot by our best works merit pardon of sin or eternal life at the hand of God, by reason of the great disproportion that is between them and the glory to come, and the infinite distance that is between us and God, whom by them we can neither profit nor satisfy for the debt of our former sins;[14] but when we have done all we can, we have done but our duty, and are unprofitable servants; and because as they are good they proceed from His Spirit,[15] and as they are wrought by us they are defiled and mixed with so much weakness and imperfection, that they cannot endure the severity of God's judgment.[16]

[14] Romans 3:20; Ephesians 2:8,9; Romans 4:6
[15] Galatians 5:22,23
[16] Isaiah 64:6; Psalm 143:2

Paragraph 6. Yet notwithstanding the persons of believers being accepted through Christ, their good works also are accepted in Him;[17] not as though they were in this life wholly unblamable and unreprovable in God's sight, but that He, looking upon them in His Son, is pleased to accept and reward that which is sincere, although accompanied with many weaknesses and imperfections.[18]

[17] Ephesians 1:5; 1 Peter 1:5
[18] Matthew 25:21,23; Hebrews 6:10

Paragraph 7. Works done by unregenerate men, although for the matter of them they may be things which God commands, and of good use both to themselves and to others;[19] yet because they proceed not from a heart purified by faith,[20] nor are done in a right manner according to the Word,[21] nor to a right end, the glory of God,[22] they are therefore sinful, and cannot please God, nor make a man meet to receive grace from God,[23] and yet their neglect of them is more sinful and displeasing to God.[24]

[19] 2 Kings 10:30; 1 Kings 21:27,29
[20] Genesis 4:5; Hebrews 11:4,6
[21] 1 Corinthians 13:1
[22] Matthew 6:2,5
[23] Amos 5:21,22; Romans 9:16; Titus 3:5
[24] Job 21:14,15; Matthew 25:41-43

CHAPTER 17

OF THE PERSEVERANCE OF THE SAINTS

Paragraph 1. Those whom God has accepted in the beloved, effectually called and sanctified by His Spirit, and given the precious faith of His elect unto, can neither totally nor finally fall from the state of grace, but shall certainly persevere therein to the end, and be eternally saved, seeing the gifts and callings of God are without repentance, from which source He still begets and nourisheth in them faith, repentance, love, joy, hope, and all the graces of the Spirit unto immortality;[1] and though many storms and floods arise and beat against them, yet they shall never be able to take them off that foundation

and rock which by faith they are fastened upon; notwithstanding, through unbelief and the temptations of Satan, the
sensible sight of the light and love of God may for a time be
clouded and obscured from them,[2] yet He is still the same, and
they shall be sure to be kept by the power of God unto salvation, where they shall enjoy their purchased possession, they
being engraven upon the palm of His hands, and their names
having been written in the book of life from all eternity.[3]

[1] John 10:28,29; Philippians 1:6; 2 Timothy 2:19; 1 John 2:19
[2] Psalm 89:31,32; 1 Corinthians 11:32
[3] Malachi 3:6

Paragraph 2. This perseverance of the saints depends not upon
their own free will, but upon the immutability of the decree
of election,[4] flowing from the free and unchangeable love of
God the Father, upon the efficacy of the merit and intercession of Jesus Christ and union with Him,[5] the oath of God,[6]
the abiding of His Spirit, and the seed of God within them,[7]
and the nature of the covenant of grace;[8] from all which ariseth also the certainty and infallibility thereof.

[4] Romans 8:30; 9:11,16
[5] Romans 5:9,10; John 14:19
[6] Hebrews 6:17,18
[7] 1 John 3:9
[8] Jeremiah 32:40

Paragraph 3. And though they may, through the temptation of
Satan and of the world, the prevalency of corruption remaining in them, and the neglect of the means of their preservation,
fall into grievous sins, and for a time continue therein,[9] whereby

they incur God's displeasure and grieve His Holy Spirit,[10] come to have their graces and comforts impaired,[11] have their hearts hardened, and their consciences wounded,[12] hurt and scandalize others, and bring temporal judgments upon themselves,[13] yet they shall renew their repentance and be preserved through faith in Christ Jesus to the end.[14]

[9] Matthew 26:70,72,74
[10] Isaiah 64:5,9; Ephesians 4:30
[11] Psalm 51:10,12
[12] Psalm 32:3,4
[13] 2 Samuel 12:14
[14] Luke 22:32,61,62

CHAPTER 18
OF THE ASSURANCE OF GRACE AND SALVATION

Paragraph 1. Although temporary believers and other unregenerate men, may vainly deceive themselves with false hopes and carnal presumptions of being in the favor of God and in a state of salvation, which hope of theirs shall perish;[1] yet such as truly believe in the Lord Jesus, and love Him in sincerity, endeavoring to walk in all good conscience before Him, may in this life be certainly assured that they are in the state of grace, and may rejoice in the hope of the glory of God,[2] which hope shall never make them ashamed.[3]

[1] Job 8:13,14; Matthew 7:22,23
[2] 1 John 2:3; 3:14,18,19,21,24; 5:13
[3] Romans 5:2,5

Paragraph 2. This certainty is not a bare conjectural and probable persuasion grounded upon a fallible hope, but an infallible assurance of faith,[4] founded on the blood and righteousness of Christ revealed in the Gospel;[5] and also upon the inward evidence of those graces of the Spirit unto which promises are made,[6] and on the testimony of the Spirit of adoption, witnessing with our spirits that we are the children of God;[7] and, as a fruit thereof, keeping the heart both humble and holy.[8]

[4] Hebrews 6:11,19
[5] Hebrews 6:17,18
[6] 2 Peter 1:4,5,10,11
[7] Romans 8:15,16
[8] 1 John 3:1-3

Paragraph 3. This infallible assurance doth not so belong to the essence of faith, but that a true believer may wait long, and conflict with many difficulties before he be partaker of it;[9] yet being enabled by the Spirit to know the things which are freely given him of God, he may, without extraordinary revelation, in the right use of means, attain thereunto:[10] and therefore it is the duty of every one to give all diligence to make his calling and election sure, that thereby his heart may be enlarged in peace and joy in the Holy Spirit, in love and thankfulness to God, and in strength and cheerfulness in the duties of obedience, the proper fruits of this assurance;[11]—so far is it from inclining men to looseness.[12]

[9] Isaiah 50:10; Psalm 88; Psalm 77:1-12
[10] 1 John 4:13; Hebrews 6:11,12
[11] Romans 5:1,2,5; 14:17; Psalm 119:32
[12] Romans 6:1,2; Titus 2:11,12,14

Paragraph 4. True believers may have the assurance of their salvation divers ways shaken, diminished, and intermitted; as by negligence in preserving of it,[13] by falling into some special sin which woundeth the conscience and grieveth the Spirit;[14] by some sudden or vehement temptation,[15] by God's withdrawing the light of His countenance, and suffering even such as fear Him to walk in darkness and to have no light,[16] yet are they never destitute of the seed of God[17] and life of faith,[18] that love of Christ and the brethren, that sincerity of heart and conscience of duty out of which, by the operation of the Spirit, this assurance may in due time be revived,[19] and by the which, in the meantime, they are preserved from utter despair.[20]

[13] Song of Solomon 5:2,3,6
[14] Psalm 51:8,12,14
[15] Psalm 116:11; 77:7,8; 31:22
[16] Psalm 30:7
[17] 1 John 3:9
[18] Luke 22:32
[19] Psalm 42:5,11
[20] Lamentations 3:26-31

CHAPTER 19
OF THE LAW OF GOD

Paragraph 1. God gave to Adam a law of universal obedience written in his heart, and a particular precept of not eating the fruit of the tree of knowledge of good and evil;[1] by which he bound him and all his posterity to personal, entire, exact, and perpetual obedience;[2] promised life upon the fulfilling, and threatened death upon the breach of it, and endued him with power and ability to keep it.[3]

[1] Genesis 1:27; Ecclesiastes 7:29
[2] Romans 10:5
[3] Galatians 3:10,12

Paragraph 2. The same law that was first written in the heart of man continued to be a perfect rule of righteousness after the fall,[4] and was delivered by God upon Mount Sinai, in ten commandments, and written in two tables, the four first containing our duty towards God, and the other six, our duty to man.[5]

[4] Romans 2:14,15
[5] Deuteronomy 10:4

Paragraph 3. Besides this law, commonly called moral, God was pleased to give to the people of Israel ceremonial laws, containing several typical ordinances, partly of worship, prefiguring Christ, His graces, actions, sufferings, and benefits;[6] and partly holding forth divers instructions of moral duties,[7] all which ceremonial laws being appointed only to the time of reformation, are, by Jesus Christ the true Messiah and only law-giver, who was furnished with power from the Father for that end, abrogated and taken away.[8]

[6] Hebrews 10:1; Colossians 2:17
[7] 1 Corinthians 5:7
[8] Colossians 2:14,16,17; Ephesians 2:14,16

Paragraph 4. To them also He gave sundry judicial laws, which expired together with the state of that people, not obliging any now by virtue of that institution; their general equity only being of moral use.[9]

  [9] 1 Corinthians 9:8-10

Paragraph 5. The moral law doth for ever bind all, as well justified persons as others, to the obedience thereof,[10] and that not only in regard of the matter contained in it, but also in respect of the authority of God the Creator, who gave it;[11] neither doth Christ in the Gospel any way dissolve, but much strengthen this obligation.[12]

  [10] Romans 13:8-10; James 2:8,10-12
  [11] James 2:10,11
  [12] Matthew 5:17-19; Romans 3:31

Paragraph 6. Although true believers be not under the law as a covenant of works, to be thereby justified or condemned,[13] yet it is of great use to them as well as to others, in that as a rule of life, informing them of the will of God and their duty, it directs and binds them to walk accordingly; discovering also the sinful pollutions of their natures, hearts, and lives, so as examining themselves thereby, they may come to further conviction of, humiliation for, and hatred against, sin;[14] together with a clearer sight of the need they have of Christ and the perfection of His obedience; it is likewise of use to the regenerate to restrain their corruptions, in that it forbids sin; and the threatenings of it serve to show what even their sins deserve, and what afflictions in this life they may expect for them, although freed from the curse and unalloyed rigor thereof. The promises of it likewise show them God's approbation of obedience, and what blessings they may expect upon the performance thereof, though not as due to them by the law as a covenant of works; so as man's doing good and refraining from evil, for the law encourageth to the one and deterreth from the other, is no evidence of his being under the law and not under grace.[15]

[13] Romans 6:14; Galatians 2:16; Romans 8:1, 10:4
[14] Romans 3:20, 7:7, etc.
[15] Romans 6:12-14; 1 Peter 3:8-13

Paragraph 7. Neither are the aforementioned uses of the law contrary to the grace of the Gospel, but do sweetly comply with it,[16] the Spirit of Christ subduing and enabling the will of man to do that freely and cheerfully which the will of God, revealed in the law, requireth to be done.[17]

[16] Galatians 3:21
[17] Ezekiel 36:27

CHAPTER 20
OF THE GOSPEL AND OF THE EXTENT OF THE GRACE THEREOF

Paragraph 1. The covenant of works being broken by sin, and made unprofitable unto life, God was pleased to give forth the promise of Christ, the seed of the woman, as the means of calling the elect, and begetting in them faith and repentance;[1] in this promise of the Gospel, as to the substance of it, was revealed, and [is] therein effectual for the conversion and salvation of sinners.[2]

[1] Genesis 3:15
[2] Revelation 13:8

Paragraph 2. This promise of Christ, and salvation by Him, is revealed only by the Word of God;[3] neither do the works of creation or providence, with the light of nature, make discovery of Christ, or of grace by Him, so much as in a general or obscure way;[4] much less that men destitute of the revelation of Him by the promise or Gospel, should be enabled thereby to attain saving faith or repentance.[5]

[3] Romans 1;17
[4] Romans 10:14,15,17
[5] Proverbs 29:18; Isaiah 25:7; 60:2,3

Paragraph 3. The revelation of the Gospel unto sinners, made in divers times and by sundry parts, with the addition of promises and precepts for the obedience required therein, as to the nations and persons to whom it is granted, is merely of the sovereign will and good pleasure of God;[6] not being annexed by virtue of any promise to the due improvement of men's natural abilities, by virtue of common light received without it, which none ever did make, or can do so;[7] and therefore in all ages, the preaching of the Gospel has been granted unto persons and nations, as to the extent or straitening of it, in great variety, according to the counsel of the will of God.

[6] Psalm 147:20; Acts 16:7
[7] Romans 1:18-32

Paragraph 4. Although the Gospel be the only outward means of revealing Christ and saving grace, and is, as such, abundantly sufficient thereunto; yet that men who are dead in trespasses may be born again, quickened or regenerated, there is moreover necessary an effectual, insuperable work of the Holy Spirit upon the whole soul, for the producing in them a new spiritual life;[8] without which no other means will effect their conversion unto God.[9]

[8] Psalm 110:3; 1 Corinthians 2:14; Ephesians 1:19,20
[9] John 6:44; 2 Corinthians 4:4,6

CHAPTER 21
OF CHRISTIAN LIBERTY
AND LIBERTY OF CONSCIENCE

Paragraph 1. The liberty which Christ hath purchased for believers under the Gospel, consists in their freedom from the guilt of sin, the condemning wrath of God, the rigor and curse of the law,[1] and in their being delivered from this present evil world,[2] bondage to Satan,[3] and dominion of sin,[4] from the evil of afflictions,[5] the fear and sting of death, the victory of the grave,[6] and everlasting damnation:[7] as also in their free access to God, and their yielding obedience unto Him, not out of slavish fear,[8] but a child-like love and willing mind.[9]

All which were common also to believers under the law for the substance of them;[10] but under the New Testament the liberty of Christians is further enlarged, in their freedom from the yoke of the ceremonial law, to which the Jewish church was subjected, and in greater boldness of access to the throne of grace, and in fuller communications of the free Spirit of God, than believers under the law did ordinarily partake of.[11]

[1] Galatians 3:13
[2] Galatians 1:4
[3] Acts 26:18
[4] Romans 8:3
[5] Romans 8:28
[6] 1 Corinthians 15:54-57
[7] 2 Thessalonians 1:10
[8] Romans 8:15;
[9] Luke 1:73-75; 1 John 4:18
[10] Galatians 3;9,14
[11] John 7:38,39; Hebrews 10:19-21

Paragraph 2. God alone is Lord of the conscience,[12] and hath left it free from the doctrines and commandments of men which are in any thing contrary to His Word, or not contained in it.[13] So that to believe such doctrines, or obey such commands out of conscience, is to betray true liberty of conscience;[14] and the requiring of an implicit faith, and absolute and blind obedience, is to destroy liberty of conscience and reason also.[15]

[12] James 4:12; Romans 14:4
[13] Acts 4:19,29; 1 Corinthians 7:23; Matthew 15:9
[14] Colossians 2:20,22,23
[15] 1 Corinthians 3:5; 2 Corinthians 1:24

Paragraph 3. They who upon pretence of Christian liberty do practice any sin, or cherish any sinful lust, as they do thereby pervert the main design of the grace of the Gospel to their own destruction,[16] so they wholly destroy the end of Christian liberty, which is, that being delivered out of the hands of all our enemies, we might serve the Lord without fear, in holiness and righteousness before Him, all the days of our lives.[17]

[16] Romans 6:1,2
[17] Galatians 5:13; 2 Peter 2:18,21

CHAPTER 22
OF RELIGIOUS WORSHIP
AND THE SABBATH DAY

Paragraph 1. The light of nature shows that there is a God, who hath lordship and sovereignty over all; is just, good and doth good to all; and is therefore to be feared, loved, praised, called upon, trusted in, and served, with all the heart and all the soul, and with all the might.[1] But the acceptable way of worshipping the true God, is instituted by Himself,[2] and so limited by His own revealed will, that He may not be worshipped according to the imagination and devices of men, nor the suggestions of Satan, under any visible representations, or any other way not prescribed in the Holy Scriptures.[3]

[1] Jeremiah 10:7; Mark 12:33
[2] Deuteronomy 12:32
[3] Exodus 20:4-6

Paragraph 2. Religious worship is to be given to God the Father, Son, and Holy Spirit, and to Him alone;[4] not to angels, saints, or any other creatures;[5] and since the fall, not without a mediator,[6] nor in the mediation of any other but Christ alone.[7]

[4] Matthew 4:9,10; John 4:23; Matthew 28:19
[5] Romans 1:25; Colossians 2:18; Revelation 19:10
[6] John 14:6
[7] 1 Timothy 2:5

Paragraph 3. Prayer, with thanksgiving, being one part of natural worship, is by God required of all men.[8] But that it may be accepted, it is to be made in the name of the Son,[9] by the help of the Spirit,[10] according to His will;[11] with understanding, reverence, humility, fervency, faith, love, and perseverance; and when with others, in a known tongue.[12]

[8] Psalm 95:1-7; 65:2
[9] John 14:13,14
[10] Romans 8:26
[11] 1 John 5:14
[12] 1 Corinthians 14:16,17

Paragraph 4. Prayer is to be made for things lawful, and for all sorts of men living, or that shall live hereafter;[13] but not for the dead,[14] nor for those of whom it may be known that they have sinned the sin unto death.[15]

[13] 1 Timothy 2:1,2; 2 Samuel 7:29
[14] 2 Samuel 12:21-23
[15] 1 John 5:16

Paragraph 5. The reading of the Scriptures,[16] preaching, and hearing the Word of God,[17] teaching and admonishing one another in psalms, hymns, and spiritual songs, singing with grace in our hearts to the Lord;[18] as also the administration of baptism,[19] and the Lord's Supper,[20] are all parts of religious worship of God, to be performed in obedience to Him, with understanding, faith, reverence, and godly fear; moreover, solemn humiliation, with fastings,[21] and thanksgivings, upon special occasions, ought to be used in an holy and religious manner.[22]

[16] 1 Timothy 4:13
[17] 2 Timothy 4:2; Luke 8:18
[18] Colossians 3:16; Ephesians 5:19
[19] Matthew 28:19,20
[20] 1 Corinthians 11:26
[21] Esther 4:16; Joel 2:12
[22] Exodus 15:1-19, Psalm 107

Paragraph 6. Neither prayer nor any other part of religious worship, is now under the Gospel, tied unto, or made more acceptable by any place in which it is performed, or towards which it is directed; but God is to be worshipped everywhere in spirit and in truth;[23] as in private families[24] daily,[25] and in secret each one by himself;[26] so more solemnly in the public assemblies, which are not carelessly nor wilfully to be neglected or forsaken, when God by His Word or providence calls thereunto.[27]

[23] John 4:21; Malachi 1:11; 1 Timothy 2:8
[24] Acts 10:2
[25] Matthew 6:11; Psalm 55:17
[26] Matthew 6:6
[27] Hebrews 10:25; Acts 2:42

Paragraph 7. As it is the law of nature, that in general a proportion of time, by God's appointment, be set apart for the worship of God, so by His Word, in a positive moral, and perpetual commandment, binding all men, in all ages, He has particularly appointed one day in seven for a sabbath to be kept holy unto Him,[28] which from the beginning of the world to the resurrection of Christ was the last day of the week, and from the resurrection of Christ was changed into the first day of the week, which is called the Lord's Day:[29] and is to be continued to the end of the world as the Christian Sabbath, the observation of the last day of the week being abolished.

[28] Exodus 20:8
[29] 1 Corinthians 16:1,2; Acts 20:7; Revelation 1:10

Paragraph 8. The sabbath is then kept holy unto the Lord, when men, after a due preparing of their hearts, and ordering their common affairs aforehand, do not only observe an holy rest all day, from their own works, words and thoughts, about their worldly employment and recreations,[30] but also are taken up the whole time in the public and private exercises of His worship, and in the duties of necessity and mercy.[31]

[30] Isaiah 58:13; Nehemiah 13:15-22
[31] Matthew 12:1-13

CHAPTER 23
OF LAWFUL OATHS AND VOWS

Paragraph 1. A lawful oath is a part of religious worship, wherein the person swearing in truth, righteousness, and judgment, solemnly calleth God to witness what he swears,[1] and to judge him according to the truth or falseness thereof.[2]

[1] Exodus 20:7; Deuteronomy 10:20; Jeremiah 4:2
[2] 2 Chronicles 6:22,23

Paragraph 2. The name of God only is that by which men ought to swear; and therein it is to be used, with all holy fear and reverence; therefore to swear vainly or rashly by that glorious and

dreadful name, or to swear at all by any other thing, is sinful,
and to be abhorred;[3] yet as in matter of weight and moment,
for confirmation of truth, and ending all strife, an oath is warranted by the Word of God;[4] so a lawful oath being imposed
by lawful authority in such matters, ought to be taken.[5]

[3] Matthew 5:34,37; James 5:12
[4] Hebrews 6:16; 2 Corinthians 1:23
[5] Nehemiah 13:25

Paragraph 3. Whosoever taketh an oath warranted by the Word
of God, ought duly to consider the weightiness of so solemn
an act, and therein to avouch nothing but what he knoweth
to be truth; for that by rash, false, and vain oaths, the Lord is
provoked, and for them this land mourns.[6]

[6] Leviticus 19:12; Jeremiah 23:10

Paragraph 4. An oath is to be taken in the plain and common
sense of the words, without equivocation or mental reservation.[7]

[7] Psalm 24:4

Paragraph 5. A vow, which is not to be made to any creature,
but to God alone, is to be made and performed with all religious care and faithfulness;[8] but popish monastical vows of
perpetual single life,[9] professed poverty,[10] and regular obedience, are so far from being degrees of higher perfection, that
they are superstitious and sinful snares, in which no Christian
may entangle himself.[11]

[8] Psalm 76:11; Genesis 28:20-22

[9] 1 Corinthians 7:2,9
[10] Ephesians 4:28
[11] Matthew 19:11

CHAPTER 24
OF THE CIVIL MAGISTRATE

Paragraph 1. God, the supreme Lord and King of all the world, hath ordained civil magistrates to be under Him, over the people, for His own glory and the public good; and to this end hath armed them with the power of the sword, for defence and encouragement of them that do good, and for the punishment of evil doers.[1]

[1] Romans 13:1-4

Paragraph 2. It is lawful for Christians to accept and execute the office of a magistrate when called thereunto; in the management whereof, as they ought especially to maintain justice and peace,[2] according to the wholesome laws of each kingdom and commonwealth, so for that end they may lawfully now, under the New Testament, wage war upon just and necessary occasions.[3]

[2] 2 Samuel 23:3; Psalm 82:3,4
[3] Luke 3:14

Paragraph 3. Civil magistrates being set up by God for the ends aforesaid; subjection, in all lawful things commanded by them, ought to be yielded by us in the Lord, not only for wrath, but for conscience' sake;[4] and we ought to make supplications and prayers for kings and all that are in authority, that under them we may live a quiet and peaceable life, in all godliness and honesty.[5]

[4] Romans 13:5-7; 1 Peter 2:17
[5] 1 Timothy 2:1,2

CHAPTER 25
OF MARRIAGE

Paragraph 1. Marriage is to be between one man and one woman; neither is it lawful for any man to have more than one wife, nor for any woman to have more than one husband at the same time.[1]

[1] Genesis 2:24; Malachi 2:15; Matthew 19:5,6

Paragraph 2. Marriage was ordained for the mutual help of husband and wife,[2] for the increase of mankind with a legitimate issue,[3] and for preventing of uncleanness.[4]

[2] Genesis 2:18
[3] Genesis 1:28
[4] 1 Corinthians 7:2,9

Paragraph 3. It is lawful for all sorts of people to marry, who are able with judgment to give their consent;[5] yet it is the duty of Christians to marry in the Lord;[6] and therefore such as profess the true religion, should not marry with infidels, or idolaters; neither should such as are godly, be unequally yoked, by marrying with such as are wicked in their life, or maintain damnable heresy.[7]

⁵ Hebrews 13:4; 1 Timothy 4:3
⁶ 1 Corinthians 7:39
⁷ Nehemiah 13:25-27

Paragraph 4. Marriage ought not to be within the degrees of consanguinity or affinity, forbidden in the Word;⁸ nor can such incestuous marriages ever be made lawful, by any law of man or consent of parties, so as those persons may live together as man and wife.⁹

⁸ Leviticus 18
⁹ Mark 6:18; 1 Corinthians 5:1

CHAPTER 26
OF THE CHURCH

Paragraph 1. The catholic or universal church, which (with respect to the internal work of the Spirit and truth of grace) may be called invisible, consists of the whole number of the elect, that have been, are, or shall be gathered into one, under Christ, the Head thereof; and is the spouse, the body, the fulness of Him that fills all in all.¹

¹ Hebrews 12:23; Colossians 1:18; Ephesians 1:10,22,23;
5:23,27,32

Paragraph 2. All persons throughout the world, professing the faith of the gospel, and obedience unto God by Christ according unto it, not destroying their own profession by any errors everting the foundation, or unholiness of conversation, are and may be called visible saints;[2] and of such ought all particular congregations to be constituted.[3]

[2] 1 Corinthians 1:2; Acts 11:26
[3] Romans 1:7; Ephesians 1:20-22

Paragraph 3. The purest churches under heaven are subject to mixture and error;[4] and some have so degenerated as to become no churches of Christ, but synagogues of Satan;[5] nevertheless Christ always hath had, and ever shall have a kingdom in this world, to the end thereof, of such as believe in Him, and make profession of His name.[6]

[4] 1 Corinthians 5; Revelation 2 and 3
[5] Revelation 18:2; 2 Thessalonians 2:11,12
[6] Matthew 16:18; Psalm 72:17; 102:28; Revelation 12:17

Paragraph 4. The Lord Jesus Christ is the Head of the church, in whom, by the appointment of the Father, all power for the calling, institution, order or government of the church, is invested in a supreme and sovereign manner;[7] neither can the Pope of Rome in any sense be head thereof, but is that antichrist, that man of sin, and son of perdition, that exalts himself in the church against Christ, and all that is called God; whom the Lord shall destroy with the brightness of His coming.[8]

[7] Colossians 1:18; Matthew 28:18-20; Ephesians 4:11,12
[8] 2 Thessalonians 2:2-9

Paragraph 5. In the execution of this power wherewith He is so intrusted, the Lord Jesus calls out of the world unto Himself, through the ministry of His Word, by His Spirit, those that

are given unto Him by His Father,[9] that they may walk before
Him in all the ways of obedience, which He prescribeth to
them in His Word.[10] Those thus called, He commandeth to
walk together in particular societies, or churches, for their
mutual edification, and the due performance of that public
worship, which He requireth of them in the world.[11]

[9] John 10:16; John 12:32
[10] Matthew 28:20
[11] Matthew 18:15-20

Paragraph 6. The members of these churches are saints by
calling, visibly manifesting and evidencing (in and by their profession and walking) their obedience unto that call of Christ;[12]
and do willingly consent to walk together, according to the
appointment of Christ; giving up themselves to the Lord, and
one to another, by the will of God, in professed subjection to
the ordinances of the Gospel.[13]

[12] Romans 1:7; 1 Corinthians 1:2
[13] Acts 2:41,42; 5:13,14; 2 Corinthians 9:13

Paragraph 7. To each of these churches thus gathered, according to His mind declared in His Word, He hath given all that
power and authority, which is in any way needful for their carrying on that order in worship and discipline, which He hath
instituted for them to observe; with commands and rules for
the due and right exerting, and executing of that power.[14]

[14] Matthew 18:17,18; 1 Corinthians 5:4,5,13; 2 Corinthians 2:6-8

Paragraph 8. A particular church, gathered and completely organized according to the mind of Christ, consists of officers and members; and the officers appointed by Christ to be chosen and set apart by the church (so called and gathered), for the peculiar administration of ordinances, and execution of power or duty, which he intrusts them with, or calls them to, to be continued to the end of the world, are bishops or elders, and deacons.[15]

[15] Acts 20:17,28; Philippians 1:1

Paragraph 9. The way appointed by Christ for the calling of any person, fitted and gifted by the Holy Spirit, unto the office of bishop or elder in a church, is, that he be chosen thereunto by the common suffrage of the church itself;[16] and solemnly set apart by fasting and prayer, with imposition of hands of the eldership of the church, if there be any before constituted therein;[17] and of a deacon that he be chosen by the like suffrage, and set apart by prayer, and the like imposition of hands.[18]

[16] Acts 14:23
[17] 1 Timothy 4:14
[18] Acts 6:3,5,6

Paragraph 10. The work of pastors being constantly to attend the service of Christ, in His churches, in the ministry of the Word and prayer, with watching for their souls, as they that must give an account to Him;[19] it is incumbent on the churches to whom they minister, not only to give them all due respect, but also to communicate to them of all their good things according to their ability,[20] so as they may have a comfortable supply, without being themselves entangled in secular affairs;[21] and may also be capable of exercising hospitality towards others;[22] and this is required by the law of nature, and by the express order of our Lord Jesus, who has ordained that they that preach the Gospel should live of the Gospel.[23]

[19] Acts 6:4; Hebrews 13:17
[20] 1 Timothy 5:17,18; Galatians 6:6,7
[21] 2 Timothy 2:4
[22] 1 Timothy 3:2
[23] 1 Corinthians 9:6-14

Paragraph 11. Although it be incumbent on the bishops or pastors of the churches, to be instant in preaching the Word, by way of office, yet the work of preaching the Word is not so peculiarly confined to them but that others also gifted and fitted by the Holy Spirit for it, and approved and called by the church, may and ought to perform it.[24]

[24] Acts 11:19-21; 1 Peter 4:10,11

Paragraph 12. As all believers are bound to join themselves to particular churches, when and where they have opportunity so to do; so all that are admitted unto the privileges of a church, are also under the censures and government thereof, according to the rule of Christ.[25]

[25] 1 Thessalonians 5:14; 2 Thessalonians 3:6,14,15

Paragraph 13. No church members, upon any offence taken by them, having performed their duty required of them towards the person they are offended at, ought to disturb any church-order, or absent themselves from the assemblies of the church, or administration of any ordinances, upon the account of such offence at any of their fellow members, but to wait upon Christ, in the further proceeding of the church.[26]

[26] Matthew 18:15-17; Ephesians 4:2,3

Paragraph 14. As each church, and all the members of it, are bound to pray continually for the good and prosperity of all the churches of Christ,[27] in all places, and upon all occasions to further it (every one within the bounds of their places and callings, in the exercise of their gifts and graces) so the churches, when planted by the providence of God, so as they may enjoy opportunity and advantage for it, ought to hold communion among themselves, for their peace, increase of love, and mutual edification.[28]

[27] Ephesians 6:18; Psalm 122:6
[28] Romans 16:1,2; 3 John 8-10

Paragraph 15. In cases of difficulties or differences, either in point of doctrine or administration, wherein either the churches in general are concerned, or any one church, in their peace, union, and edification; or any member or members of any church are injured, in or by any proceedings in censures not agreeable to truth and order: it is according to the mind of Christ, that many churches holding communion together, do, by their messengers, meet to consider, and give their advice in or about that matter in difference, to be reported to all the churches concerned;[29] howbeit these messengers assembled, are not intrusted with any church-power properly so called; or with any jurisdiction over the churches themselves, to exercise any censures either over any churches or persons; or to impose their determination on the churches or officers.[30]

[29] Acts 15:2,4,6,22,23,25
[30] 2 Corinthians 1:24; 1 John 4:1

CHAPTER 27
OF THE COMMUNION OF THE SAINTS

Paragraph 1. All saints that are united to Jesus Christ, their Head, by His Spirit, and faith, although they are not made thereby one person with Him, have fellowship in His graces, sufferings, death, resurrection, and glory;[1] and, being united to one another in love, they have communion in each other's gifts and graces,[2] and are obliged to the performance of such duties, public and private, in an orderly way, as do conduce to their mutual good, both in the inward and outward man.[3]

[1] 1 John 1:3; John 1:16; Philippians 3:10; Romans 6:5,6
[2] Ephesians 4:15,16; 1 Corinthians 12:7; 3:21-23
[3] 1 Thessalonians 5:11,14; Romans 1:12; 1 John 3:17,18; Galatians 6:10

Paragraph 2. Saints by profession are bound to maintain an holy fellowship and communion in the worship of God, and in performing such other spiritual services as tend to their mutual edification;[4] as also in relieving each other in outward things according to their several abilities, and necessities;[5] which communion, according to the rule of the Gospel, though especially to be exercised by them, in the relation wherein they stand, whether in families,[6] or churches,[7] yet, as God offereth opportunity, is to be extended to all the household of faith, even all those who in every place call upon the name of the Lord Jesus; nevertheless their communion one with another as saints, doth not take away or infringe the title or propriety which each man hath in his goods and possessions.[8]

[4] Hebrews 10:24,25; 3:12,13
[5] Acts 11:29,30
[6] Ephesians 6:4
[7] 1 Corinthians 12:14-27
[8] Acts 5:4; Ephesians 4:28

CHAPTER 28
OF BAPTISM AND THE LORD'S SUPPER

Paragraph 1. Baptism and the Lord's Supper are ordinances of positive and sovereign institution, appointed by the Lord Jesus, the only Lawgiver, to be continued in His church to the end of the world.[1]

[1] Matthew 28:19,20; 1 Corinthians 11:26

Paragraph 2. These holy appointments are to be administered by those only who are qualified and thereunto called, according to the commission of Christ.[2]

[2] Matthew 28:19; 1 Corinthians 4:1

· CHAPTER 29
OF BAPTISM

Paragraph 1. Baptism is an ordinance of the New Testament, ordained by Jesus Christ, to be unto the party baptized, a sign of his fellowship with Him, in His death and resurrection; of his being engrafted into Him;[1] of remission of sins;[2] and of giving up unto God, through Jesus Christ, to live and walk in newness of life.[3]

[1] Romans 6:3-5; Colossians 2:12; Galatians 3:27
[2] Mark 1:4; Acts 22:16
[3] Romans 6:2,4

Paragraph 2. Those who do actually profess repentance towards God, faith in, and obedience to, our Lord Jesus Christ, are the only proper subjects of this ordinance.[4]

[4] Mark 16:16; Acts 8:36,37

Paragraph 3. The outward element to be used in this ordinance is water, wherein the party is to be baptized, in the name of the Father, and of the Son, and of the Holy Spirit.[5]

[5] Matthew 28:19, 20; Acts 8:38

Paragraph 4. Immersion, or dipping of the person in water, is necessary to the due administration of this ordinance.[6]

[6] Matthew 3:16; John 3:23

CHAPTER 30
OF THE LORD'S SUPPER

Paragraph 1. The Supper of the Lord Jesus was instituted by Him the same night wherein He was betrayed, to be observed in His churches, unto the end of the world, for the perpetual remembrance, and showing to all the world the sacrifice of Himself in His death,[1] confirmation of the faith of believers in all the benefits thereof, their spiritual nourishment, and growth in Him, their further engagement in, and to all duties which they owe to Him; and to be a bond and pledge of their communion with Him, and with each other.[2]

[1] 1 Corinthians 11:23-26
[2] 1 Corinthians 10:16,17,21

Paragraph 2. In this ordinance Christ is not offered up to His Father, nor any real sacrifice made at all for remission of sin of the quick or dead, but only a memorial of that one offering up of Himself by Himself upon the cross, once for all;[3] and a spiritual oblation of all possible praise unto God for the same.[4] So that the popish sacrifice of the mass, as they call it, is most abominable, injurious to Christ's own sacrifice the alone propitiation for all the sins of the elect.

[3] Hebrews 9:25,26,28
[4] 1 Corinthians 11:24; Matthew 26:26,27

Paragraph 3. The Lord Jesus hath, in this ordinance, appointed His ministers to pray, and bless the elements of bread and wine, and thereby to set them apart from a common to a holy use, and to take and break the bread; to take the cup, and, they communicating also themselves, to give both to the communicants.[5]

[5] 1 Corinthians 11:23-26

Paragraph 4. The denial of the cup to the people, worshipping the elements, the lifting them up, or carrying them about for adoration, and reserving them for any pretended religious use, are all contrary to the nature of this ordinance, and to the institution of Christ.[6]

[6] Matthew 26:26-28; 15:9; Exodus 20:4,5

Paragraph 5. The outward elements in this ordinance, duly set apart to the use ordained by Christ, have such relation to Him crucified, as that truly, although in terms used figuratively, they are sometimes called by the names of the things they represent, in other words, the body and blood of Christ,[7] albeit, in substance and nature, they still remain truly and only bread and wine, as they were before.[8]

[7] 1 Corinthians 11:27
[8] 1 Corinthians 11:26-28

Paragraph 6. That doctrine which maintains a change of the substance of bread and wine, into the substance of Christ's body and blood, commonly called transubstantiation, by consecration of a priest, or by any other way, is repugnant not to Scripture alone,[9] but even to common sense and reason, overthrows the nature of the ordinance, and has been, and is, the cause of manifold superstitions, yea, of gross idolatries.[10]

[9] Acts 3:21; Luke 14:6,39
[10] 1 Corinthians 11:24,25

Paragraph 7. Worthy receivers, outwardly partaking of the visible elements in this ordinance, do then also inwardly by faith, really and indeed, yet not carnally and corporally, but spiritually receive, and feed upon Christ crucified, and all the benefits of His death; the body and blood of Christ being then not corporally or carnally, but spiritually present to the faith of believers in that ordinance, as the elements themselves are to their outward senses.[11]

[11] 1 Corinthians 10:16; 11:23-26

Paragraph 8. All ignorant and ungodly persons, as they are unfit to enjoy communion with Christ, so are they unworthy of the Lord's Table, and cannot, without great sin against Him, while they remain such, partake of these holy mysteries, or be admitted thereunto;[12] yea, whosoever shall receive unworthily, are guilty of the body and blood of the Lord, eating and drinking judgment to themselves.[13]

[12] 2 Corinthians 6:14,15
[13] 1 Corinthians 11:29; Matthew 7:6

CHAPTER 31

OF THE STATE OF MAN AFTER DEATH, AND OF THE RESURRECTION OF THE DEAD

Paragraph 1. The bodies of men after death return to dust, and see corruption;[1] but their souls, which neither die nor sleep, having an immortal subsistence, immediately return to God who gave them.[2] The souls of the righteous being then made perfect in holiness, are received into paradise, where they are

with Christ, and behold the face of God in light and glory,
waiting for the full redemption of their bodies;[3] and the souls
of the wicked are cast into hell; where they remain in torment
and utter darkness, reserved to the judgment of the great day;[4]
besides these two places, for souls separated from their bodies,
the Scripture acknowledgeth none.

[1] Genesis 3:19; Acts 13:36
[2] Ecclesiastes 12:7
[3] Luke 23:43; 2 Corinthians 5:1,6,8; Philippians 1:23; Hebrews 12:23
[4] Jude 6, 7; 1 Peter 3:19; Luke 16:23,24

Paragraph 2. At the last day, such of the saints as are found
alive, shall not sleep, but be changed;[5] and all the dead shall be
raised up with the selfsame bodies, and none other;[6] although
with different qualities, which shall be united again to their
souls forever.[7]

[5] 1 Corinthians 15:51,52; 1 Thessalonians 4:17
[6] Job 19:26,27
[7] 1 Corinthians 15:42,43

Paragraph 3. The bodies of the unjust shall, by the power of
Christ, be raised to dishonor; the bodies of the just, by His
Spirit, unto honor, and be made conformable to His own glo-
rious body.[8]

[8] Acts 24:15; John 5:28,29; Philippians 3:21

CHAPTER 32
OF THE LAST JUDGMENT

Paragraph 1. God hath appointed a day wherein He will judge the world in righteousness, by Jesus Christ;[1] to whom all power and judgment is given of the Father; in which day, not only the apostate angels shall be judged,[2] but likewise all persons that have lived upon the earth shall appear before the tribunal of Christ, to give an account of their thoughts, words, and deeds, and to receive according to what they have done in the body, whether good or evil.[3]

[1] Acts 17:31; John 5:22,27
[2] 1 Corinthians 6:3; Jude 6
[3] 2 Corinthians 5:10; Ecclesiastes 12:14; Matthew 12:36; Romans 14:10,12; Matthew 25:32-46

Paragraph 2. The end of God's appointing this day, is for the manifestation of the glory of His mercy, in the eternal salvation of the elect; and of His justice, in the eternal damnation of the reprobate, who are wicked and disobedient;[4] for then shall the righteous go into everlasting life, and receive that fulness of joy and glory with everlasting rewards, in the presence of the Lord; but the wicked, who do not know God, and do not obey the Gospel of Jesus Christ, shall be cast aside into everlasting torments,[5] and punished with everlasting destruction, from the presence of the Lord, and from the glory of His power.[6]

[4] Romans 9:22,23
[5] Matthew 25:21,34; 2 Timothy 4:8
[6] Matthew 25:46; Mark 9:48; 2 Thessalonians 1:7-10

Paragraph 3. As Christ would have us to be certainly persuaded that there shall be a Day of Judgment, both to deter all men from sin,[7] and for the greater consolation of the godly in their adversity,[8] so will He have the day unknown to men, that they may shake off all carnal security, and be always watchful, because they know not at what hour the Lord will come,[9] and may ever be prepared to say, *Come Lord Jesus; come quickly.*[10] Amen.

[7] 2 Corinthians 5:10,11
[8] 2 Thessalonians 1:5-7
[9] Mark 13:35-37; Luke 12:35-40
[10] Revelation 22:20

ENDING STATEMENT AND SIGNATORIES

We the MINISTERS, and MESSENGERS of, and concerned for upwards of, one hundred BAPTIZED CHURCHES, in England and Wales (denying Arminianisim), being met together in London, from the third of the seventh month to the eleventh of the same, 1689, to consider of some things that might be for the glory of God, and the good of these congregations, have thought meet (for the satisfaction of all other Christians that differ from us in the point of Baptism) to recommend to their perusal the confession of our faith, which confession we own, as containing the doctrine of our faith and practice, and do desire that the members of our churches respectively do furnish themselves therewith.

Hansard Knollys, Pastor, Broken Wharf, London
William Kiffin, Pastor, Devonshire-square, London
John Harris, Pastor, Joiner's Hall, London
William Collins, Pastor, Petty France, London
Hurcules Collins, Pastor, Wapping, London
Robert Steed, Pastor, Broken Wharf, London
Leonard Harrison, Pastor, Limehouse, London
George Barret, Pastor, Mile End Green, London
Isaac Lamb, Pastor, Pennington-street, London
Richard Adams, Minister, Shad Thames, Southwark
Benjamin Keach, Pastor, Horse-lie-down, Southwark
Andrew Gifford, Pastor, Bristol, Fryars, Som. & Glouc.
Thomas Vaux, Pastor, Broadmead, Som. & Glouc.
Thomas Winnel, Pastor, Taunton, Som. & Glouc.
James Hitt, Preacher, Dalwood, Dorset
Richard Tidmarsh, Minister, Oxford City, Oxon
William Facey, Pastor, Reading, Berks
Samuel Buttall, Minister, Plymouth, Devon

Christopher Price, Minister, Abergayenny, Monmouth
Daniel Finch, Minister, Kingsworth, Herts
John Ball, Minister, Tiverton, Devon
Edmond White, Pastor, Evershall, Bedford
William Prichard, Pastor, Blaenau, Monmouth
Paul Fruin, Minister, Warwick, Warwick
Richard Ring, Pastor, Southhampton, Hants
John Tomkins, Minister, Abingdon, Berks
Toby Willes, Pastor, Bridgewater, Somerset
John Carter, Pastor, Steventon, Bedford
James Webb, Pastor, Devizes, Wilts
Richard Sutton, Pastor, Tring, Herts
Robert Knight, Pastor, Stukeley, Bucks
Edward Price, Pastor, Hereford City, Hereford
William Phipps, Pastor, Exon, Devon
William Hawkins, Pastor, Dimmock, Gloucester
Samuel Ewer, Pastor, Hemstead, Herts
Edward Man, Pastor, Houndsditch, London
Charles Archer, Pastor, Hock-Norton, Oxon

In the name of and on the behalf of the whole assembly.

AN APPENDIX ON BAPTISM

Whosoever reads, and impartially considers what we have in our forgoing confession declared, may readily perceive, that we do not only consent with all other true Christians on the Word of God (revealed in the Scriptures of truth) as the foundation and rule of our faith and worship. But that we have also industriously endeavored to manifest, that in the fundamental articles of Christianity we mind the same things, and have therefore expressed our belief in the same words, that have on the like occasion been spoken by other societies of Christians before us.

This we have done, that those who are desirous to know the principles of religion which we hold and practice, may take an estimate from our selves (who jointly concur in this work) and may not be misguided, either by undue reports; or by the ignorance or errors of particular persons, who going under the same name with ourselves, may give an occasion of scandalizing the truth we profess.

And although we do differ from our brethren who are paedobaptists; in the subject and administration of baptism, and such other circumstances as have a necessary dependence on our observance of that ordinance, and do frequent our own assemblies for our mutual edification, and discharge of those duties, and services which we owe unto God, and in His fear to each other: yet we would not be from this misconstrued, as if the discharge of our own consciences herein, did in any way disoblige or alienate our affections, or conversation from any others that fear the Lord; but that we may and do as we have opportunity participate of the labors of those, whom God hath endued with abilities above ourselves, and qualified, and called to the ministry of the Word, earnestly desiring to approve ourselves to be such, as follow after peace with holiness, and therefore we always keep that blessed *Irenicum,* or healing Word of the Apostle before our eyes; "if in anything ye be other-wise minded, God shall reveal even this unto you; nevertheless whereto we have already attained; let us walk by the same rule, let us mind the same thing" (Philippians 3:15,16).

Let it not therefore be judged of us (because much hath been written on this subject, and yet we continue this our practice different from others) that it is out of obstinacy, but rather as the truth is, that we do herein according to the best of our understandings worship God, out of a pure mind yielding obedience to His precept, in that method which we take to be most agreeable to the Scriptures of truth, and primitive practice.

It would not become us to give any such intimation, as should carry a semblance that what we do in the service of God is with a doubting conscience, or with any such temper of mind that we do thus for the present, with a reservation that we will do otherwise hereafter upon more mature delib-eration; nor have we any cause so to do, being fully persuaded, that what we do is agreeable to the will of God. Yet we do heartily propose this, that if any of the servants of our Lord Jesus shall, in the spirit of meekness, attempt to convince us of any mistake either in judgment or practice, we shall diligently ponder his arguments; and account him our chiefest friend that shall be an instrument to convert us from any error that is in our ways, for we cannot wittingly do anything against the truth, but all things for the truth.

And therefore we have endeavored seriously to consider, what has been already offered for our satisfaction in this point; and are loath to say any more lest we should be esteemed desirous of renewed contests about them: yet forasmuch as it may justly be expected that we show some reason, why we cannot acquiesce in what has been urged against us; we shall with as much brevity as may consist with plainness, endeavor to satisfy the expectation of those that shall peruse what we now publish in this matter also.

1. As to those Christians who consent with us, *That Repentance from dead works, and Faith towards God, and our Lord Jesus Christ, is required in persons to be Baptized*; and do therefore supply the defect of the (infant being incapable of making confession of either) by others who do undertake these things for it. Although we do find by Church history that this hath been a very ancient practice; yet considering, that the same Scripture which does caution us against censuring our brother, with whom we shall all stand before the judgment seat of Christ, does also instruct us, *That every one of us shall give an account of himself to God* (Romans 14:4,10,12), and *whatsoever is not of Faith is Sin* (Romans 14:23). Therefore we cannot for our own parts be persuaded in our own minds, to build such a practice as this, upon an unwritten tradition: but do rather choose in all points of faith and worship, to have recourse to the Holy Scriptures, for the information of our judgment, and regula-

tion of our practice; being well assured that a conscientious attending unto, is the best way to prevent, and rectify our defects and errors (2 Timothy 3:16,17). And if any such case happen to be debated between Christians, which is not plainly determinable by the Scriptures, we think it safest to leave such things undecided until the second coming of our Lord Jesus; as they did in the Church of old, until there should arise a priest with *Urim* and *Thummim*, that might certainly inform them of the mind of God thereabout (Ezra 2:62,63).

2. As for those our Christian brethren who do ground their arguments for infants baptism, upon a presumed federal Holiness, or church-membership, we conceive they are deficient in this, that albeit this covenant-holiness and membership should be as is supposed, in reference unto the infants of believers; yet no command for infant baptism does immediately and directly result from such a quality, or relation.

All instituted Worship receives its sanction from the precept, and is to be thereby governed in all the necessary circumstances thereof.

So it was in the covenant that God made with Abraham and his seed. The sign whereof was appropriated only to the male, notwithstanding that the female seed as well as the male were comprehended in the covenant and part of the church of God; neither was this sign to be affixed to any male infant till he was eight days old, albeit he was within the covenant from the first moment of his life; nor could the danger of death, or any other supposed necessity, warrant the circumcising of him before the set time, nor was there any cause for it; the punishment of being cut off from his people, being only upon the neglect, or contempt of the precept.

Righteous Lot was nearly related to Abraham in the flesh, and contemporary with him, when this Covenant was made; yet inasmuch as he did not descend from his loins, nor was of his household family (although he was of the same household of faith with *Abraham*) yet neither Lot himself nor any of his posterity (because of their descent from him) were signed with the signature of this Covenant that was made with Abraham and his seed.

This may suffice to show, that where there was both an express covenant, and a sign thereof (such a covenant as did separate the persons with whom it was made, and all their offspring from all the rest of the world, as a people holy unto the Lord, and did constitute them the visible church of God, though not comprehensive of all the faithful in the world) yet the sign of this covenant was not affixed to all the persons that were within this covenant, nor to any of them till the appointed season; nor to other faithful servants of God, that were not of descent from Abraham. And consequently that it depends purely upon the will of the Lawgiver, to determine what shall be the sign of His covenant, unto whom, at what season, and upon what terms, it shall be affixed.

If our brethren do suppose baptism to be the seal of the covenant which God makes with every believer (of which the Scriptures are altogether silent) it is not our concern to contend with them herein; yet we conceive the seal of that covenant is the indwelling of the Spirit of Christ in the particular and individual persons in whom He resides, and nothing else, neither do they or we suppose that baptism is in any such manner substituted in the place of circumcision, as to have the same (and no other) latitude, extent, or terms, then circumcision had; for that was suited only for the male children, baptism is an ordinance suited for every believer, whether male, or female. That extended to all the males that were born in Abraham's house, or bought with his money, equally with the males that proceeded from his own loins; but baptism is not so far extended in any true Christian church that we know of, as to be administered to all the poor infidel servants, that the members thereof purchase for their service, and introduce into their families; nor to the children born of them in their house.

But we conceive the same parity of reasoning may hold for the ordinance of baptism as for that of circumcision; i.e. one law for the stranger, as for the home born (Exodus 12:49): If any desire to be admitted to all the ordinances, and privileges of God's house, the door is open; upon the same terms that any one person was ever admitted to all, or any of those privileges, that belong to the Christian church; may all persons of right challenge the like admission.

As for that text of Scripture, Romans 4:11, "He received circumcision a seal of the righteousness of the faith which he had yet being uncircumcised;" we conceive if the Apostle's scope in that place be duly attended to, it will appear that no argument can be taken from there to enforce infant baptism; and forasmuch as we find a full and fair account of those words given by the learned Dr. Lightfoot (a man not to be suspected of partiality in this controversy) in his *Horae Hebrai*, on the

1 Corinthians 7:19 (pp. 42, 43), we shall transcribe his words at large, without any comment of our own upon them.

> Circumcision is nothing, if we respect the time, for now it was without use, that end of it being especially fulfilled; for which it had been instituted: this end the Apostle declares in these words, Romans 4:11 σφραγιδα etc. But I fear that by most translations they are not sufficiently suited to the end of circumcision, and the scope of the Apostle whilst something of their own is by them inserted.

And after the Doctor hath represented diverse versions of the words agreeing for the most part in sense with that which we have in our Bibles, he thus proceeds.

> Other versions are to the same purpose; as if circumcision was given to Abraham for a Seal of that Righteousness which he had being yet uncircumcised, which we will not deny to be in some sense true, but we believe that circumcision had chiefly a far different respect.
>
> Give me leave thus to render the words; And he received the sign of circumcision, a seal of the Righteousness of Faith, which was to be in the uncircumcision, Which was to be (I say) not which had been, not that which Abraham had whilst he was yet uncircumcised; but that which his uncircumcised seed should have, that is the Gentiles, who in time to come should imitate the faith of Abraham.
>
> Now consider well on what occasion circumcision was instituted unto Abraham, setting before thine eyes the history thereof, Genesis 17.
>
> This promise is first made unto him, Thou shalt be the Father of many Nations (in what sense the Apostle explaineth in that chapter) and then there is subjoined a double seal for the confirmation of the thing, to wit, the change of the name

Abram into Abraham, and the institution of circumcision. v. 4. Behold as for me, my Covenant is with thee, and thou shalt be the Father of many Nations. Wherefore was his name called Abraham? for the sealing of this promise. Thou shalt be the Father of many Nations. And wherefore was circumcision instituted to him? For the sealing of the same promise. Thou shalt be the Father of many Nations. So that this is the sense of the Apostle; most agreeable to the institution of circumcision; he received the sign of circumcision, a seal of the Righteousness of Faith which in time to come the uncircumcision (or the Gentiles) should have and obtain.

Abraham had a twofold seed, natural, of the Jews; and faithful, of the believing Gentiles: his natural seed was signed with the sign of circumcision, first indeed for the distinguishing of them from all other Nations whilst they as yet were not the seed of Abraham, but especially for the memorial of the justification of the Gentiles by faith, when at length they should become his seed. Therefore circumcision was of right to cease, when the Gentiles were brought in to the faith, forasmuch as then it had obtained its last and chief end, & thenceforth circumcision is nothing.

Thus far he, which we earnestly desire may be seriously weighed, for we plead not his authority, but the evidence of truth in his words.

3. Of whatsoever nature the holiness of the children mentioned, 1 Corinthians 7:12. be, yet they who do conclude that all such children (whether infants or of riper years) have from hence an immediate right to baptism, do as we conceive put more into the conclusion, then will be found in the premises.

For although we do not determine positively concerning the Apostle's scope in the holiness here mentioned, so as to say it is this, or that, and no other thing; yet it is evident that the Apostle does by it determine not only the lawfulness but the expedience also of a believer's cohabitation with an unbeliever, in the state of marriage.

And we do think that although the Apostle's asserting of the unbelieving yokefellow to be sanctified by the believer, should carry in it somewhat more than is in the bare marriage of two infidels, because although the marriage covenant has a divine sanction so as to make the wedlock of two unbelievers a lawful action, and their conjunction and cohabitation in that respect undefiled, yet there might be no ground to suppose from this that both or either of their persons are thereby sanctified; and the Apostle urges the cohabitation of a believer with an infidel in the state of wedlock from this ground that the unbelieving husband is sanctified by the believing wife; nevertheless here you have the influence of a believer's faith ascending from an inferior to a superior relation; from the wife to the husband who is her head, before it can descend to their offspring. And therefore we say, whatever be the nature or extent of the holiness here intended, we conceive it cannot convey to the children an immediate right to baptism; because it would then be of another nature, and of a larger extent, then the root, and original from whence it is derived, for it is clear by the Apostle's argument that holiness cannot be derived to the child from the sanctity of one parent only, if either father or mother be (in the sense intended by the Apostle) unholy or unclean, so will the child be also, therefore for the production of an holy seed it is necessary that both the parents be sanctified; and this the Apostle positively asserts in the first place to be done by the believing parent, although the other be an unbeliever; and then consequentially from thence argues, the holiness of their children. Hence it follows, that as the children have no other holiness then what they derive from both their parents; so neither can they have any right by this holiness to any spiritual privilege but such as both their parents did also partake of: and therefore if the unbelieving parent (though sanctified by the believing parent) have not thereby a right to baptism, neither can we conceive, that there is any such privilege, derived to the children by their birth-holiness.

Besides if it had been the usual practice in the apostle's days for the father or mother that did believe, to bring all their children with them to be baptized; then the holiness of the believing Corinthians' children, would not at all have been in question when this epistle was written; but might have been argued from their passing under that ordinance, which represented their new birth, although they had derived no holiness from their parents, by their first birth; and would have lain as an exception against the Apostle's inference, "else were your children unclean..." But of the sanctification of all the children of every believer by this ordinance, or any other way, then what is before mentioned, the Scripture is altogether silent.

This may also be added; that if this birth-holiness does qualify all the children of every believer, for the ordinance of baptism; why not for all other ordinances? For the Lord's

Supper as was practiced for a long time together. For if recourse be had to what the Scriptures speak generally of this subject; it will be found that the same qualities which do entitle any person to baptism, do so also for the participation of all the ordinances, and privileges of the house of God, that are common to all believers.

Whosoever can and does interrogate his good conscience towards God when he is baptized (as everyone must do that makes it to himself a sign of salvation) is capable of doing the same thing, in every other act of worship that he performs.

4. The arguments and inferences that are usually brought for, or against infant baptism from those few instances which the Scriptures afford us of whole families being baptized; are only conjectural; and therefore cannot of themselves, be conclusive on either hand: yet in regard most that treat on this subject for infant baptism, do (as they conceive) improve these instances to the advantage of their argument: we think it meet (in like manner as in the cases before mentioned so in this) to show the invalidity of such inferences.

"Cornelius worshipped God with all his house," the Jailer, and Crispus the chief ruler of the Synagogue, "believed God with each of their houses." "The household of Stephanus addicted themselves to the Ministry of the Saints:" so that thus far worshipping, and believing runs parallel with baptism. And if Lydia, had been a married person, when she believed, it is probable her husband would also have been named by the Apostle, as in like cases, inasmuch as he would have been not only a part, but the head of that baptized household.

Who can assign any probable reason, why the Apostle should make mention of four or five households being baptized and no more or why he does so often vary in the method of his salutations (cf. Romans 1:6), sometimes mentioning only particular persons of great note, other times such, and the church in their house? The saints that were with them; and them belonging to Narcissus, who were in the Lord; thus saluting either whole families, or part of families, or only particular persons in families, considered as they were in the Lord, for if it had been an usual practice to baptize all children, with their parents; there were then many thousands of the Jews which believed, and a great number of the Gentiles, in most of the principle cities in the world, and among so many thousands, it is more then probable there would have been some thousands of households baptized; why then should the Apostle in this respect signalize one family of the Jews and three or four of the Gentiles, as particular instances in a case that was common? Whoever supposes that we do willfully debar our children, from the benefit of any promise, or privilege, that of right belongs to the children of believing parents; they do entertain over severe thoughts of us: to be without natural affections is one of the characters of the worst of persons; in the worst of times. We do freely confess ourselves guilty before the Lord, in that we have not with more circumspection and diligence trained up those that relate to us in the fear of the Lord; and do humbly and earnestly pray, that our omissions herein may be remitted, and that they may not redound to the prejudice of ourselves, or any of ours: but with respect to that duty that is incumbent on us, we acknowledge ourselves obliged by the precepts of God, to bring up our children in the nurture and admonition of the Lord, to teach them His fear, both by instruction and example; and should we set light by this precept, it would demonstrate that we are more vile then the unnatural heathen, that like not to retain God in their knowledge, our baptism might then be justly accounted, as no baptism to us.

There are many special promises that do encourage us as well as precepts, that do oblige us to the close pursuit of our duty herein: that God whom we serve, being jealous of His worship, threatens the visiting of the father's transgression upon the children to the third and fourth generation of them that hate Him: yet does more abundantly extend His mercy, even to thousands (respecting the offspring and succeeding generations) of them that love Him, and keep His commands.

When our Lord rebuked His disciples for prohibiting the access of little children that were brought to Him, that He might pray over them, lay His hands upon them, and bless them, does declare, "that of such is the Kingdom of God." And the Apostle Peter in answer to their enquiry, that desired to know what they must do to be saved, does not only instruct them in the necessary duty of repentance and baptism; but does also thereto encourage them, by that promise which had reference both to them, and their children; if our Lord Jesus in the forementioned place, do not respect the qualities of children (as elsewhere) as to their meekness, humility, and sincerity, and the like; but intend also that those very persons and such like, appertain to the Kingdom of God, and if the Apostle Peter in mentioning the aforesaid promise, do respect not only the present and succeeding generations of those Jews, that heard him, (in which sense the same phrase does occur in Scripture) but also the immediate offspring of his auditors; whether the promise relate to the gift of the Holy Spirit, or of eternal life, or any grace, or privilege tending to the obtaining thereof; it is neither our concern nor our interest to confine the mercies, and promises of God, to a more narrow, or lesser compass than He is pleased graciously to offer and intend them; nor to have a light esteem of them; but are obliged in duty to God, and affection to our children; to plead earnestly with God and use our utmost endeavors that both our selves, and our offspring may be partakers of His mercies and gracious promises: yet we cannot from either of these texts collect a sufficient warrant for us to baptize our children before they are instructed in the principles of the Christian religion.

For as to the instance in little children, it seems by the disciples forbidding them, that they were brought upon some other account, not so frequent as Baptism must be supposed to have been, if from the beginning believers' children had been admitted thereto: and no account is given whether their parents were baptized believers or not; and as to the instance of the Apostle; if the following words and practice, may be taken as an interpretation of the scope of that promise we cannot conceive it does refer to infant baptism, because the text does presently subjoin; "Then they that gladly received the word were baptized."

That there were some believing children of believing parents in the Apostles' days is evident from the Scriptures, even such as were then in their father's family, and under their parents tuition, and education; to whom the Apostle in several of his epistles to the churches, gives commands to obey their parents in the Lord; and does allure their tender years to hearken to this precept, by reminding them that it is the first command with promise.

And it is recorded by him for the praise of Timothy, and encouragement of parents betimes to instruct, and children early to attend to godly instruction, that $\alpha\pi o$ $\beta\rho\epsilon\phi o\varsigma$ "from a child," he had known the Holy Scriptures.

The Apostle John rejoiced greatly when he found of the children of the Elect Lady walking in the truth; and the children of her Elect Sister join with the Apostle in his salutation.

But that this was not generally so, that all the children of believers were accounted for believers (as they would have been if they had been all baptized) may be collected from the character which the Apostle gives of persons fit to be chosen to eldership in the church which was not common to all believers; among others this is expressly one, i.e. "If there be any having believing, or faithful children," not accused of riot or unruly; and we may from the Apostle's writings on the same subject collect the reason of this qualification, i.e., that in case the person designed for this office to teach and rule in the house of God, had children capable of it; there might be first a proof of his ability, industry, and success in this work in his own family; and private capacity, before he was ordained to the exercise of this authority in the church, in a public capacity, as a bishop in the house of God.

These things we have mentioned as having a direct reference unto the controversy between our brethren and us; other
things that are more abstruse and prolix, which are frequently
introduced into this controversy, but do not necessarily concern it, we have purposely avoided; that the distance between
us and our brethren may not be by us made more wide; for it
is our duty, and concern so far as is possible for us (retaining
a good conscience towards God) to seek a more entire agreement and reconciliation with them.

We are not insensible that as to the order of God's house,
and entire communion therein there are some things wherein
we (as well as others) are not at a full accord among ourselves, as for instance; the known principle, and state of the
consciences of diverse of us, that have agreed in this Confession is such; that we cannot hold church-communion, with
any other then baptized believers, and churches constituted
of such; yet some others of us have a greater liberty and
freedom in our spirits that way; and therefore we have purposely omitted the mention of things of that nature, that we
might concur, in giving this evidence of our agreement, both
among our selves, and with other good Christians, in those
important articles of the Christian religion, mainly insisted
on by us: and this notwithstanding we all esteem it our chief
concern, both among ourselves, and all others that in every
place call upon the name of the Lord Jesus Christ our Lord,
both theirs and ours, and love Him in sincerity, to endeavor
to keep the unity of the Spirit, in the bond of peace; and in
order thereunto, to exercise all lowliness and meekness, with
long-suffering, forbearing one another in love.

And we are persuaded if the same method were introduced into frequent practice between us and our Christian friends who agree with us in all the fundamental articles of the Christian faith (though they do not so in the subject and administration of baptism) it would soon beget a better understanding, and brotherly affection between us.

In the beginning of the Christian church, when the doctrine of the baptism of Christ was not universally understood, yet those that knew only the baptism of John, were the disciples of the Lord Jesus; and Apollos an eminent minister of the Gospel of Jesus.

In the beginning of the reformation of the Christian church, and recovery from that Egyptian darkness wherein our forefathers for many generations were held in bondage; upon recourse had to the Scriptures of truth, different apprehensions were conceived, which are to this time continued, concerning the practice of this ordinance.

Let not our zeal herein be misinterpreted: that God whom we serve is jealous of His worship. By His gracious providence the Law thereof, is continued amongst us; and we are forewarned by what happened in the Church of the Jews, that it is necessary for every generation, and that frequently in every generation to consult the divine oracle, compare our worship with the rule, and take heed to what doctrines we receive and practice.

If the Ten Commands exhibited in the popish idolatrous service books had been received as the entire Law of God, because they agree in number with his ten commands, and also in the substance of nine of them; the second commandment forbidding idolatry had been utterly lost.

If Ezra and Nehemiah had not made a diligent search into the particular parts of God's law, and His worship; the Feast of Tabernacles (which for many centuries of years, had not been duly observed, according to the institution, though it was retained in the general notion) would not have been kept in due order.

So may it be now as to many things relating to the service of God, which do retain the names proper to them in their first institution, but yet through inadvertency (where there is no sinister design) may vary in their circumstances, from their first institution. And if by means of any ancient defection, or of that general corruption of the service of God, and interruption of His true worship, and persecution of His servants by the Antichristian Bishop of Rome, for many generations; those who do consult the Word of God, cannot yet arrive at a full and mutual satisfaction among themselves, what was the practice of the primitive Christian Church, in some points relating to the Worship of God: yet inasmuch as these things are not of the essence of Christianity, but that we agree in the fundamental doctrines thereof, we do apprehend, there is sufficient ground to lay aside all bitterness and prejudice, and in the spirit of love and meekness to embrace and own each other therein; leaving each other at liberty to perform such other services, (wherein we cannot concur) apart unto God, according to the best of our understanding.

FINIS

FOREWORD TO THE
BAPTIST CATECHISM

James M. Renihan

The 'faith once for all delivered to the saints' (Jude 3) may be expressed in a variety of ways. A good confession communicates it systematically. Moving from foundational topics through the whole spectrum of belief, it presents doctrine in all of its interrelated beauty. Another way of stating the faith is by means of questions and answers, that is, catechetically. This method is especially useful for memorization. Christians have used it for millennia.

When the Westminster Assembly sought to further the reformation of the Church of England in the 1640s, it employed both of these means. A *Confession of Faith* was produced, becoming the basis for the convictions of millions of Reformed Christians. The Assembly also produced two catechisms. The *Larger Catechism* is a detailed learning device for theology; but more famous is the *Shorter Catechism* they published. The puritan pastor Thomas Vincent said 'I know no catechism more full of light and sound doctrine', and he was not alone in his evaluation. Our Baptist fathers recognized the profound benefit found in its careful expressions, and knew that it could be of great benefit in their own churches. For this reason, at their 1693 General Assembly, they determined 'That a Catechism be drawn up, containing the substance of the Christian religion, for the instruction of children and servants, and that brother William Collins be desired to draw it up.' When this project was delayed, the Western churches, meeting in Bristol wrote to their London brothers and said

> Moreover [we] desire you will remember your agreement at your last assembling, and minuted in the narrative, that brother Collins should draw up a catechism, and that it should be printed, a thing so needful and useful that the country have been longing to have it, and are troubled at the delay of it, and earnestly desire that you will hasten the printing of it. They suppose that the greatness of the number that will be sold will pay the cost. There had need be thousands of them printed, pray let it be done, and sent abroad to the churches. They think you cannot do anything that will be of more general use.

This is high praise and encouragement! So far as these men were concerned, the advance of the Christian Faith would be profoundly aided (nothing could be better!) by the adaptation and publication of a *Baptist* catechism. In fact, they believed that *thousands* of copies should be distributed.

It has been suggested that William Collins was an editor of the Baptist Confession. This is buttressed here. Perhaps his skill in doing that work indicated that he was a natural choice for this work as well (his co-elder, Nehemiah Coxe, had died early in 1689). In any case, we know that soon after the work was completed and published. By 1695 it was in its fifth edition, and by 1703 in its 10th edition. Curiously, the earliest known copy in existence is the 5th edition, but this may be because they were intended for use in families. Perhaps they were so well used they were worn out.

For those familiar with the Westminster *Shorter Catechism*, the Baptist edition will be immediately recognizable. With only minor alterations to the doctrine of baptism, it provides a wonderful method by which parents, children, teachers and students may learn, memorize and live out Christian doctrine. It is a great joy to join together with our fathers in the faith and recite together the deep truths of our common doctrinal heritage. In this way, we may fulfill the apostolic command to contend for this faith 'once for all delivered.'

James M. Renihan
Escondido, CA
May 2010

THE BAPTIST CATECHISM

Q. 1: Who is the first and chiefest being?
A. God is the first and chiefest being.[1]

   [1] Isaiah 44:6; 48:12; Psalm 97:9

Q. 2: Ought everyone to believe there is a God?
A. Everyone ought to believe there is a God;[1] and it is their great sin and folly who do not.[2]

   [1] Hebrews 11:6
   [2] Psalm 14:1

Q. 3: How may we know there is a God?
A. The light of nature in man and the works of God plainly declare there is a God;[1] but His Word and Spirit only do it fully and effectually for the salvation of sinners.[2]

   [1] Romans 1:19,20; Psalm 19:1-3; Acts 17:24
   [2] 1 Corinthians 2:10; 2 Timothy 3:15,16

Q. 4: What is the Word of God?
A. The Holy Scriptures of the Old and New Testament are the Word of God, and the only certain rule of faith and obedience.[1]

   [1] 2 Timothy 3:16; Ephesians 2:20

Q. 5: May all men make use of the Holy Scriptures?
A. All men are not only permitted, but commanded and exhorted to read, hear, and understand the Holy Scriptures.[1]

   [1] John 5:38; Revelation 22:18,19; 1:3; Acts 8:30

Q. 6: What things are chiefly contained in the Holy Scriptures?
A. The Holy Scriptures chiefly contain what man ought to believe concerning God, and what duty God requireth of man.[1]

   [1] 2 Timothy 1:13; 3:15,16

Q. 7: What is God?
A. God is a Spirit,[1] infinite,[2] eternal,[3] and unchangeable[4] in His being,[5] wisdom,[6] power,[7] holiness,[8] justice, goodness, and truth.[9]

   [1] John 4:24
   [2] Job 11:7,8,9
   [3] Psalm 90:2
   [4] James 1:17
   [5] Exodus 3:14
   [6] Psalm 147:5
   [7] Revelation 4:8
   [8] Revelation 15:4
   [9] Exodus 34:6

Q. 8: Are there more gods than one?
A. There is but one only, the living and true God.[1]

   [1] Deuteronomy 6:4; Jeremiah 10:10

Q. 9: How many persons are there in the Godhead?
A. There are three persons in the Godhead, the Father, the Son, and the Holy Spirit; and these three are one God, the same in essence, equal in power and glory.[1]

   [1] 1 John 5:7; Matthew 28:19; Genesis 1:1-3; John 1:1-3; Hebrews 1:1-3; John 17:5

Q. 10: What are the decrees of God?
A. The decrees of God are His eternal purpose according to the counsel of His will, whereby, for His own glory, He hath foreordained whatsoever comes to pass.[1]

> [1] Ephesians 1:4,11; Romans 9:22-23; Isaiah 46:10;
> Lamentations 3:37

Q. 11: How doth God execute His decrees?
A. God executeth His decrees in the works of creation and providence.

Q. 12: What is the work of creation?
A. The work of creation is God's making all things of nothing, by the word of His power, in the space of six days, and all very good.[1]

> [1] Genesis 1 throughout; Hebrews 11:3

Q. 13: How did God create man?
A. God created man, male and female, after His own image, in knowledge, righteousness, and holiness, with dominion over the creatures.[1]

> [1] Genesis 1:26-28; Colossians 3:10; Ephesians 4:24

Q. 14: What are God's works of providence?
A. Gods works of providence are His most holy,[1] wise,[2] and powerful preserving[3] and governing all His creatures, and all their actions.[4]

> [1] Psalm 145:17
> [2] Psalm 104:24; Isaiah 28:29

[3] Hebrews 1:3
[4] Psalm 103:19; Matthew 10:29-31

Q. 15: What special act of providence did God exercise towards man in the estate wherein he was created?

A. When God had created man, He entered into a covenant of life with him upon condition of perfect obedience: forbidding him to eat of the tree of the knowledge of good and evil, upon pain of death.[1]

[1] Galatians 3:12; Genesis 2:17

Q. 16: Did our first parents continue in the estate wherein they were created?

A. Our first parents being left to the freedom of their own will, fell from the estate wherein they were created, by sinning against God.[1]

[1] Genesis 3:6-8,13; Ecclesiastes 7:29

Q. 17: What is sin?

A. Sin is any want of conformity unto, or transgression of, the law of God.[1]

[1] 1 John 3:4

Q. 18: What was the sin whereby our first parents fell from the estate wherein they were created?

A. The sin whereby our parents fell from the estate wherein they were created, was their eating the forbidden fruit.[1]

[1] Genesis 3:6,12

Q. 19: Did all mankind fall in Adam's first transgression?
A. The covenant being made with Adam, not only for himself but for his posterity, all mankind descending from him by ordinary generation sinned in him, and fell with him in his first transgression.[1]

[1] Genesis 2:16,17; Romans 5:12; 1 Corinthians 15:21,22

Q. 20: Into what estate did the fall bring mankind?
A. The fall brought mankind into an estate of sin and misery.[1]

[1] Romans 5:12

Q. 21: Wherein consists the sinfulness of that estate whereinto man fell?
A. The sinfulness of that estate whereinto man fell, consists in the guilt of Adam's first sin, the want of original righteousness, and the corruption of his whole nature, which is commonly called original sin; together with all actual transgressions which proceed from it.[1]

[1] Romans 5:12, to the end; Ephesians 2:1-3; James 1:14,15;
   Matthew 15:19

Q. 22: What is the misery of that estate whereinto man fell?
A. All mankind by their fall lost communion with God,[1] are under His wrath and curse,[2] and so made liable to all miseries in this life, to death itself, and to the pains of hell for ever.[3]

[1] Genesis 3:8,10,24
[2] Ephesians 2:2,3; Galatians 3:10
[3] Lamentations 3:39; Romans 6:23; Matthew 25:41,46

Q. 23: Did God leave all mankind to perish in the estate of sin and misery?

A. God having out of His mere good pleasure, from all eternity, elected some to everlasting life,[1] did enter into a covenant of grace, to deliver them out of the estate of sin and misery, and to bring them into an estate of salvation by a Redeemer.[2]

[1] Ephesians 1:4,5
[2] Romans 3:20-22; Galatians 3:21,22

Q. 24: Who is the Redeemer of God's elect?

A. The only Redeemer of God's elect is the Lord Jesus Christ;[1] who, being the eternal Son of God, became man,[2] and so was and continueth to be God and man in two distinct natures, and one person for ever.[3]

[1] 1 Timothy 2:5,6
[2] John 1:14; Galatians 4:4
[3] Romans 9:5; Luke 1:35; Colossians 2:9; Hebrews 7:24,25

Q. 25: How did Christ, being the Son of God become man?

A. Christ the Son of God became man by taking to Himself a true body,[1] and a reasonable soul;[2] being conceived by the power of the Holy Spirit in the womb of the Virgin Mary, and born of her,[3] yet without sin.[4]

[1] Hebrews 2:14,16; 10:5
[2] Matthew 26:38
[3] Luke 1:27,31,34,35,42; Galatians 4:4
[4] Hebrews 4:15; 7:26

Q. 26: What offices doth Christ execute as our Redeemer?

A. Christ as our Redeemer executeth the offices of a

prophet, of a priest, and of a king, both in His state of humiliation and exaltation.[1]

[1] Acts 3:22; Hebrews 12:25; 2 Corinthians 13:3; Hebrews 5:5-7;
Psalm 2:6; Isaiah 9:6,7; Matthew 21:5; Psalm 2:8-11

Q. 27: How doth Christ execute the office of a prophet?
A. Christ executeth the office of a prophet in revealing to us, by His Word and Spirit, the will of God for our salvation.[1]

[1] John 1:18; 2 Peter 1:10-12; John 15:15; and 20:31

Q. 28: How doth Christ execute the office of a priest?
A. Christ executeth the office of a priest in His once offering up Himself a sacrifice to satisfy divine justice[1] and reconcile us to God,[2] and in making continual intercession for us.[3]

[1] Hebrews 9:14,28
[2] Hebrews 2:17
[3] Hebrews 7:24,25

Q. 29: How doth Christ execute the office of a king?
A. Christ executeth the office of a king, in subduing us to Himself,[1] in ruling,[2] and defending us,[3] and in restraining and conquering all His and our enemies.[4]

[1] Acts 15:14-16
[2] Isaiah 33:22
[3] Isaiah 32:1,2
[4] 1 Corinthians 15:25; Psalm 110 throughout

Q. 30: Wherein did Christ's humiliation consist?
A. Christ's humiliation consisted in His being born, and that

in a low condition,[1] made under the law,[2] undergoing the miseries of this life,[3] the wrath of God,[4] and the cursed death of the cross;[5] in being buried,[6] and continuing under the power of death for a time.[7]

[1] Luke 2:7
[2] Galatians 4:4
[3] Hebrews 12:2,3; Isaiah 53:2,3
[4] Luke 22:44; Matthew 27:46
[5] Philippians 2:8
[6] 1 Corinthians 15:4
[7] Acts 2:24-27,31; Matthew 12:40

Q. 31: Wherein consisteth Christ's exaltation?
A. Christ's exaltation consisteth in His rising again from the dead on the third day,[1] in ascending up into heaven,[2] in sitting at the right hand of God the Father,[3] and in coming to judge the world at the last day.[4]

[1] 1 Corinthians 15:4
[2] Mark 16:19
[3] Ephesians 1:20
[4] Acts 1:11; 17:31

Q. 32: How are we made partakers of the redemption purchased by Christ?
A. We are made partakers of the redemption purchased by Christ, by the effectual application of it to us[1] by His Holy Spirit.[2]

[1] John 1:11-13
[2] Titus 3:5,6

Q. 33: How doth the Spirit apply to us the redemption purchased by Christ?
A. The Spirit applieth to us the redemption purchased by Christ, by working faith in us,[1] and thereby uniting us to Christ, in our effectual calling.[2]

[1] Ephesians 1:13,14; John 6:37,39; Ephesians 2:8
[2] Ephesians 3:17; 1 Corinthians 1:9

Q. 34: What is effectual calling?
A. Effectual calling is the work of God's Spirit,[1] whereby convincing us of our sin and misery,[2] enlightening our minds in the knowledge of Christ,[3] and renewing our wills,[4] He doth persuade and enable us to embrace Jesus Christ freely offered to us in the Gospel.[5]

[1] 2 Timothy 1:9; 2 Thessalonians 2:13,14
[2] Acts 2:37
[3] Acts 26:18
[4] Ezekiel 36:26,27
[5] John 6:44,45; Philippians 2:13

Q. 35: What benefits do they that are effectually called partake of in this life?
A. They that are effectually called do in this life partake of justification,[1] adoption,[2] sanctification, and the several benefits which in this life do either accompany or flow from them.[3]

[1] Romans 8:30
[2] Ephesians 1:5
[3] 1 Corinthians 1:30

Q. 36: What is justification?

A. Justification is an act of God's free grace, wherein He pardoneth all our sins,[1] and accepteth us as righteous in His sight,[2] only for the righteousness of Christ imputed to us,[3] and received by faith alone.[4]

   [1] Romans 3:24,25; and 4:6-8
   [2] 2 Corinthians 5:19,21
   [3] Romans 5:17-19
   [4] Galatians 2:16; Philippians 3:9

Q. 37: What is adoption?

A. Adoption is an act of God's free grace,[1] whereby we are received into the number and have a right to all the privileges of the sons of God.[2]

   [1] 1 John 3:1
   [2] John 1:12; Romans 8:14

Q. 38: What is sanctification?

A. Sanctification is the work of God's free grace,[1] whereby we are renewed in the whole man after the image of God,[2] and are enabled more and more to die unto sin, and live unto righteousness.[3]

   [1] 2 Thessalonians 2:13
   [2] Ephesians 4:23,24
   [3] Romans 6:4,6

Q. 39: What are the benefits which in this life do accompany or flow from justification, adoption, and sanctification?

A. The benefits which in this life do accompany or flow from justification, adoption, and sanctification, are assurance of God's love, peace of conscience,[1] joy in the Holy Spirit,[2] increase of grace,[3] and perseverance therein to the end.[4]

[1] Romans 5:1,2,5
[2] Romans 5:5,17
[3] Proverbs 4:18
[4] 1 John 5:13; 1 Peter 1:5

Q. 40: What benefits do believers receive from Christ at their death?

A. The souls of believers are at their death made perfect in holiness,[1] and do immediately pass into glory;[2] and their bodies being still united to Christ,[3] do rest in their graves,[4] till the resurrection.[5]

[1] Hebrews 12:23
[2] 2 Corinthians 5:1,6,8; Philippians 1:23; Luke 23:43
[3] 1 Thessalonians 4:14
[4] Isaiah 57:2
[5] Job 19:26,27

Q. 41: What benefits do believers receive from Christ at the resurrection?

A. At the resurrection believers, being raised up in glory,[1] shall be openly acknowledged, and acquitted in the Day of Judgment,[2] and made perfectly blessed, both in soul and body, in the full enjoyment of God[3] to all eternity.[4]

[1] 1 Corinthians 15:43
[2] Matthew 25:23; Matthew 10:32
[3] 1 John 3:2; 1 Corinthians 13:12
[4] 1 Thessalonians 4:17,18

Q. 42: But what shall be done to the wicked at their death?
A. The souls of the wicked shall, at their death, be cast into the torments of hell, and their bodies lie in their graves, till the resurrection and judgment of the great day.[1]

[1] Luke 16:23,24; Acts 1:25; Jude 7; 1 Peter 3:19; Psalm 49:14

Q. 43: What shall be done to the wicked, at the Day of Judgment?
A. At the Day of Judgment the bodies of the wicked, being raised out of their graves, shall be sentenced, together with their souls, to unspeakable torments with the devil and his angels for ever.[1]

[1] John 5:28,29; Matthew 25:41,46; 2 Thessalonians 1:8,9

Q. 44: What is the duty which God requireth of man?
A. The duty which God requireth of man, is obedience to His revealed will.[1]

[1] Micah 6:8; 1 Samuel 15:22

Q. 45: What did God at first reveal to man for the rule of his obedience?
A. The rule which God at first revealed to man for his obedience, was the moral law.[1]

[1] Romans 2:14,15, and 10:5

Q. 46: Where is the moral law summarily comprehended?
A. The moral law is summarily comprehended in the Ten Commandments.[1]

[1] Deuteronomy 10:4; Matthew 19:17-19

Q. 47: What is the sum of the Ten Commandments?
A. The sum of the Ten Commandments is, to love the Lord our God, with all our heart, with all our soul, with all our strength, and with all our mind; and our neighbor as ourselves.[1]

[1] Matthew 22:37-40

Q. 48: What is the preface to the Ten Commandments?
A. The preface to the Ten Commandments is in these words; I am the Lord thy God which have brought thee out of the land of Egypt, out of the house of bondage.[1]

[1] Exodus 20:2

Q. 49: What doth the preface to the Ten Commandments teach us?
A. The preface to the Ten Commandments teacheth us that because God is the Lord, and our God and Redeemer, therefore we are bound to keep all His commandments.[1]

[1] Luke 1:74,75; 1 Peter 1:15-19

Q. 50: Which is the first commandment?
A. The first commandment is, Thou shalt have no other gods before Me.[1]

[1] Exodus 20:3

Q. 51: What is required in the first commandment?
A. The first commandment requireth us to know and acknowledge God to be the only true God and our God;[1] and to worship and glorify Him accordingly.[2]

[1] 1 Chronicles 28:9; Deuteronomy 26:17
[2] Matthew 4:10; Psalm 29:2

Q. 52: What is forbidden in the first commandment?
A. The first commandment forbiddeth the denying,[1] or not
worshipping and glorifying the true God,[2] as God and our
God,[3] and the giving that worship and glory to any other,
which is due unto Him alone.[4]

[1] Psalm 14:1
[2] Romans 1:21
[3] Psalm 81:10,11
[4] Romans 1:25,26

*Q. 53: What are we especially taught by these words "before Me,"
in the first commandment?*
A. These words "before Me," in the first commandment
teach us, that God, who seeth all things, taketh notice of and
is much displeased with the sin of having any other god.[1]

[1] Ezekiel 8:5-18

Q. 54: Which is the second commandment?
A. The second commandment is, Thou shalt not make unto
thee any graven image, or the likeness of anything that is
in heaven above, or that is in the earth beneath, or that is
in the water under the earth; thou shalt not bow down thy-
self to them, nor serve them: for I the Lord thy God am
a jealous God, visiting the iniquity of the fathers upon the
children unto the third and fourth generation of them that
hate Me; and shewing mercy unto thousands of them that
love Me, and keep My commandments.[1]

[1] Exodus 20:4-6

Q. 55: What is required in the second commandment?
A. The second commandment requireth the receiving, observing, and keeping pure and entire all such religious worship and ordinances, as God hath appointed in His Word.[1]

[1] Deuteronomy 32:46; Matthew 28:20; Acts 2:42

Q. 56: What is forbidden in the second commandment?
A. The second commandment forbiddeth the worshipping of God by images,[1] or any other way not appointed in His Word.[2]

[1] Deuteronomy 4:15-19; Exodus 32:5,8
[2] Deuteronomy 12:31,32

Q. 57: What are the reasons annexed to the second commandment?
A. The reasons annexed to the second commandment are, God's sovereignty over us,[1] His propriety in us,[2] and the zeal He hath to His own worship.[3]

[1] Psalm 95:2,3,6
[2] Psalm 45:11
[3] Exodus 34:13,14

Q. 58: Which is the third commandment?
A. The third commandment is, Thou shalt not take the name of the Lord thy God in vain; for the Lord will not hold him guiltless that taketh His name in vain.

[1] Exodus 20:7

Q. 59: What is required in the third commandment?
A. The third commandment requireth the holy and reverent

use of God's names,[1] titles,[2] attributes,[3] ordinances,[4] word,[5]
and works.[6]

[1] Matthew 6:9; Deuteronomy 28:58
[2] Psalm 68:4
[3] Revelation 15:3,4
[4] Malachi 1:11,14
[5] Psalm 138:1,2
[6] Job 36:24

Q. 60: What is forbidden in the third commandment?
A. The third commandment forbiddeth all profaning and
abusing of anything whereby God makes Himself known.[1]

[1] Malachi 1:6,7,12; 2:2; 3:14

Q. 61: What is the reason annexed to the third commandment?
A. The reason annexed to the third commandment is, that
however the breakers of this commandment may escape
punishment from men, yet the Lord our God will not suffer
them to escape His righteous judgment.[1]

[1] 1 Samuel 2:12,17,22,24,29; 3:13; Deuteronomy 28:58,59

Q. 62: What is the fourth commandment?
A. The fourth commandment is, Remember the Sabbath
day to keep it holy: six days shalt thou labour and do all thy
work; but the seventh day is the Sabbath of the Lord thy
God, in it thou shalt not do any work, thou, nor thy son,
nor thy daughter, nor thy man-servant, nor thy maid-servant,
nor thy cattle, nor the stranger that is within thy gates: for
in six days the Lord made heaven and earth, the sea, and all

that in them is, and rested the seventh day; wherefore the Lord blessed the Sabbath day and hallowed it.[1]

[1] Exodus 20:8-11

Q. 63: What is required in the fourth commandment?
A. The fourth commandment requireth the keeping holy to God one whole day in seven to be a Sabbath to Himself.

[1] Exodus 20:8-11; Deuteronomy 5:12-14

Q. 64: Which day of the seven hath God appointed to be the weekly Sabbath?
A. Before the resurrection of Christ, God appointed the seventh day of the week to be the weekly Sabbath;[1] and the first day of the week ever since, to continue to the end of the world, which is the Christian Sabbath.[2]

[1] Exodus 20:8-11; Deuteronomy 5:12-14
[2] Psalm 118:24; Matthew 28:1; Mark 2:27,28; 16:2; Luke 24:1,30-36; John 20:1,19-21,26; Acts 1:3; 2:1,2; 20:7; 1 Corinthians 16:1,2; Revelation 1:10

Q. 65: How is the Sabbath to be sanctified?
A. The Sabbath is to be sanctified by a holy resting all that day,[1] even from such worldly employments and recreations as are lawful on other days;[2] and spending the whole time in the public and private exercises of God's worship,[3] except so much as is to be taken up in the works of necessity and mercy.[4]

[1] Exodus 20:8,10
[2] Exodus 16:25-28; Nehemiah 13:15-22
[3] Luke 4:16; Acts 20:7; Psalm 92:title; Isaiah 66:23
[4] Matthew 12:1-13

Q. 66: What is forbidden in the fourth commandment?
A. The fourth commandment forbiddeth the omission or careless performance of the duties required,[1] and the profaning the day by idleness,[2] or doing that which is in itself sinful,[3] or by unnecessary thoughts, words, or works, about worldly employments or recreations.[4]

[1] Ezekiel 22:26; Amos 8:5; Malachi 1:13
[2] Acts 20:7,9
[3] Ezekiel 23:38
[4] Jeremiah 17:24-27; Isaiah 58:13

Q. 67: What are the reasons annexed to the fourth commandment?
A. The reasons annexed to the fourth commandment, are God's allowing us six days of the week for our own lawful employments,[1] His challenging a special propriety in a seventh, His own example, and His blessing the Sabbath day.[2]

[1] Exodus 20:9
[2] Exodus 20:11

Q. 68: Which is the fifth commandment?
A. The fifth commandment is, Honor thy father and thy mother; that thy days may be long in the land which the Lord thy God giveth thee.[1]

[1] Exodus 20:12

Q. 69: What is required in the fifth commandment?
A. The fifth commandment requireth the preserving the honor and performing the duties belonging to everyone in their several places and relations, as superiors,[1] inferiors,[2] or equals.[3]

[1] Ephesians 5:21
[2] 1 Peter 2:17
[3] Romans 12:10

Q. 70: What is forbidden in the fifth commandment?
A. The fifth commandment forbiddeth the neglect of, or doing anything against the honor and duty which belongeth to everyone in their several places and relations.[1]

[1] Matthew 15:4-6; Ezekiel 34:2-4; Romans 13:8

Q. 71: What is the reason annexed to the fifth commandment?
A. The reason annexed to the fifth commandment is a promise of long life and prosperity (as far as it shall serve for God's glory, and their own good) to all such as keep this commandment.[1]

[1] Deuteronomy 5:16; Ephesians 6:2,3

Q. 72: What is the sixth commandment?
A. The sixth commandment is, Thou shalt not kill.[1]

[1] Exodus 20:13

Q. 73: What is required in the sixth commandment?
A. The sixth commandment requireth all lawful endeavors to preserve our own life[1] and the life of others.[2]

[1] Ephesians 5:28,29
[2] 1 Kings 18:4

Q. 74: What is forbidden in the sixth commandment?
A. The sixth commandment absolutely forbiddeth the taking

away of our own life, or the life of our neighbor unjustly, or whatsoever tendeth thereunto.[1]

[1] Acts 16:28; Genesis 9:6

Q. 75: Which is the seventh commandment?
A. The seventh commandment is, Thou shalt not commit adultery.[1]

[1] Exodus 20:14

Q. 76: What is required in the seventh commandment?
A. The seventh commandment requireth the preservation of our own and our neighbor's chastity, in heart, speech, and behavior.[1]

[1] 1 Corinthians 7:2,3,5,34,36; Colossians 4:6; 1 Peter 3:2

Q. 77: What is forbidden in the seventh commandment?
A. The seventh commandment forbiddeth all unchaste thoughts, words, and actions.[1]

[1] Matthew 15:19; 5:28; Ephesians 5:3,4

Q. 78: Which is the eighth commandment?
A. The eighth commandment is, Thou shalt not steal.[1]

[1] Exodus 20:15

Q. 79: What is required in the eighth commandment?
A. The eighth commandment requireth the lawful procuring and furthering the wealth and outward estate of ourselves and others.[1]

[1] Genesis 30:30; 1 Timothy 5:8; Leviticus 25:35; Deuteronomy 22:1-5; Exodus 23:4,5; Genesis 47:14,20

Q. 80: What is forbidden in the eighth commandment?
A. The eighth commandment forbiddeth whatsoever doth or may unjustly hinder our own[1] or our neighbor's wealth or outward estate.[2]

  [1] 1 Timothy 5:8; Proverbs 28:19
  [2] Proverbs 21:17; 23:20,21; 28:19; Ephesians 4:28

Q. 81: Which is the ninth commandment?
A. The ninth commandment is, Thou shalt not bear false witness against thy neighbor.[1]

  [1] Exodus 20:16

Q. 82: What is required in the ninth commandment?
A. The ninth commandment requireth the maintaining and promoting of truth between man and man,[1] and of our own and our neighbor's good name,[2] especially in witness bearing.[3]

  [1] Zechariah 8:16
  [2] 3 John 12
  [3] Proverbs 14:5,25

Q. 83: What is forbidden in the ninth commandment?
A. The ninth commandment forbiddeth whatsoever is prejudicial to truth, or injurious to our own or our neighbor's good name.[1]

  [1] 1 Samuel 17:28; Leviticus 19:16; Psalm 15:3

Q. 84: Which is the tenth commandment?
A. The tenth commandment is Thou shalt not covet thy neighbor's house, thou shalt not covet thy neighbor's wife,

nor his man-servant, nor his maid-servant, nor his ox, nor his ass, nor anything that is thy neighbor's.[1]

[1] Exodus 20:17

Q. 85: *What is required in the tenth commandment?*
A. The tenth commandment requireth full contentment with our own condition,[1] with a right and charitable frame of spirit toward our neighbor, and all that is his.[2]

[1] Hebrews 13:5; 1 Timothy 6:6
[2] Job 31:29; Romans 12:15; 1 Timothy 1:5; 1 Corinthians 13:4,7

Q. 86: *What is forbidden in the tenth commandment?*
A. The tenth commandment forbiddeth all discontentment with our own estate,[1] envying or grieving at the good of our neighbor,[2] and all inordinate motions and affections to anything that is his.[3]

[1] 1 Kings 21:4; Esther 5:13; 1 Corinthians 10:10
[2] Galatians 5:26; James 3:14,16
[3] Romans 7:7,8; 13:9; Deuteronomy 5:21

Q. 87: *Is any man able perfectly to keep the commandments of God?*
A. No mere man since the fall is able in this life perfectly to keep the commandments of God,[1] but doth daily break them in thought, word, or deed.[2]

[1] Ecclesiastes 7:20; 1 John 1:8,10; Galatians 5:17
[2] Genesis 6:5; 8:21; Romans 3:9-21; James 3:2-13

Q. 88: *Are all transgressions of the law equally heinous?*
A. Some sins in themselves, and by reason of several aggravations, are more heinous in the sight of God than others.[1]

[1] Ezekiel 8:6,13,15; 1 John 5:16; Psalm 78:17,32,56

Q. 89: What doth every sin deserve?

A. Every sin deserveth God's wrath and curse, both in this life and that which is to come.[1]

[1] Ephesians 5:6; Galatians 3:10; Lamentations 3:39;
    Matthew 25:41; Romans 6:23

Q. 90: What doth God require of us that we may escape His wrath and curse, due to us for sin?

A. To escape the wrath and curse of God due to us for sin, God requireth of us faith in Jesus Christ, repentance unto life,[1] with the diligent use of all the outward means whereby Christ communicateth to us the benefits of redemption.[2]

[1] Acts 20:21
[2] Proverbs 2:1-6, 8:33-36; Isaiah 55:2,3

Q. 91: What is faith in Jesus Christ?

A. Faith in Jesus Christ is a saving grace,[1] whereby we receive and rest upon Him alone for salvation, as He is offered to us in the Gospel.[2]

[1] Hebrews 10:39
[2] John 1:12; Isaiah 26:3,4; Philippians 3:9; Galatians 2:16

Q. 92: What is repentance unto life?

A. Repentance unto life is a saving grace,[1] whereby a sinner, out of a true sense of his sin,[2] and apprehension of the mercy of God in Christ,[3] doth, with grief and hatred of his sin, turn from it unto God,[4] with full purpose of and endeavor after new obedience.[5]

[1] Acts 11:28
[2] Acts 2:37,38

[3] Joel 2:12; Jeremiah 3:22
[4] Jeremiah 31:18,19; Ezekiel 36:31
[5] 2 Corinthians 7:11; Isaiah 1:16,17

Q. 93: What are the outward means whereby Christ communicateth to us the benefits of redemption?
A. The outward and ordinary means whereby Christ communicateth to us the benefits of redemption are His ordinances, especially the Word, baptism, the Lord's Supper, and prayer; all which means are made effectual to the elect for salvation.[1]

[1] Matthew 28:19,20; Acts 2:42,46,47

Q. 94: How is the Word made effectual to salvation?
A. The Spirit of God maketh the reading, but especially the preaching of the Word, an effectual means of convincing and converting sinners, and of building them up in holiness and comfort through faith unto salvation.[1]

[1] Nehemiah 8:8; Acts 26:18; Psalm 19:8; Acts 20:32;
    Romans 1:15,16; 10:13-17; 15:4; 1 Corinthians 14:24,25;
    1 Timothy 3:15-17

Q. 95: How is the Word to be read and heard, that it may become effectual to salvation?
A. That the Word may become effectual to salvation, we must attend thereunto with diligence,[1] preparation,[2] and prayer;[3] receive it with faith and love,[4] lay it up in our hearts,[5] and practice it in our lives.[6]

[1] Proverbs 8:34
[2] 1 Peter 2:1,2
[3] Psalm 119:18

⁴ Hebrews 4:2; 2 Thessalonians 2:10
⁵ Psalm 119:11
⁶ Luke 8:15; James 1:25

Q. 96: How do baptism and the Lords Supper become effectual means of salvation?
A. Baptism and the Lords Supper become effectual means of salvation, not for any virtue in them, or in him that doth administer them, but only by the blessing of Christ,¹ and the working of the Spirit in those that by faith receive them.²

¹ 1 Peter 3:21; Matthew 3:11; 1 Corinthians 3:6,7
² 1 Corinthians 12:3

Q. 97: What is baptism?
A. Baptism is an ordinance of the New Testament instituted by Jesus Christ,¹ to be unto the party baptized a sign of his fellowship with Him, in His death, burial, and resurrection; of his being engrafted into Him;² of remission of sins;³ and of his giving up himself unto God through Jesus Christ, to live and walk in newness of life.⁴

¹ Matthew 28:19
¹ Romans 6:3-5; Colossians 2:12; Galatians 3:27
² Mark 1:4; Acts 2:38; 22:16
³ Romans 6:3,4

Q. 98: To whom is baptism to be administered?
A. Baptism is to be administered to all those who actually profess repentance toward God, faith in and obedience to our Lord Jesus Christ, and to none other.¹

¹ Matthew 3:6; 28:19; Mark 16:16; Acts 2:37,38; 8:36-38

Q. 99: Are the infants of such as are professing believers to be baptized?
A. The infants of such as are professing believers are not to be baptized, because there is neither command or example in the Holy Scriptures, or certain consequence from them to baptize such.[1]

[1] Proverbs 30:6; Luke 3:7,8

Q. 100: How is baptism rightly administered?
A. Baptism is rightly administered by immersion, or dipping the whole body of the party in water, into the name of the Father, and of the Son, and of the Holy Spirit, according to Christ's institution, and the practice of the apostles,[1] and not by sprinkling or pouring of water, or dipping some part of the body, after the tradition of men.

[1] Matthew 3:16; John 3:23; Matthew 28:19,20; Acts 8:38; 10:48; Romans 6:4; Colossians 2:12

Q. 101: What is the duty of such who are rightly baptized?
A. It is the duty of such who are rightly baptized to give up themselves to some particular and orderly church of Jesus Christ, that they may walk in all the commandments and ordinances of the Lord blameless.[1]

[1] Acts 2:41,42; 5:13,14; 9:26; 1 Peter 2:5; Luke 1:6

Q. 102: What is the Lord's Supper?
A. The Lord's Supper is an ordinance of the New Testament, instituted by Jesus Christ; wherein by giving and receiving bread and wine, according to His appointment, His death is

shown forth, and the worthy receivers are, not after a corporal and carnal manner, but by faith, made partakers of His body and blood, with all His benefits, to their spiritual nourishment and growth in grace.[1]

[1] Matthew 26:26-28; 1 Corinthians 11:23-26; 10:16

Q. 103: Who are the proper subjects of this ordinance?
A. They who have been baptized upon a personal profession of their faith in Jesus Christ, and repentance from dead works.[1]

[1] Acts 2:41,42

Q. 104: What is required to the worthy receiving of the Lord's Supper?
A. It is required of them that would worthily partake of the Lord's Supper, that they examine themselves of their knowledge to discern the Lord's body,[1] of their faith to feed upon Him,[2] of their repentance,[3] love,[4] and new obedience,[5] lest coming unworthily they eat and drink judgment to themselves.[6]

[1] 1 Corinthians 11:28,29
[2] 2 Corinthians 13:5
[3] 1 Corinthians 11:31
[4] 1 Corinthians 10:16,17
[5] 1 Corinthians 5:7,8
[6] 1 Corinthians 11:28,29

Q. 105: What is prayer?
A. Prayer is an offering up our desires to God,[1] by the assistance of the Holy Spirit,[2] for things agreeable to His will,[3] in

the name of Christ,[4] believing,[5] with confession of our sins,[6] and thankful acknowledgments of His mercies.[7]

  [1] Psalm 62:8
  [2] Romans 8:26
  [3] 1 John 5:14; Romans 8:27
  [4] John 16:23
  [5] Matthew 21:22; James 1:6
  [6] Psalm 32:5,6; Daniel 9:4
  [7] Philippians 4:6

Q. 106: What rule hath God given for our direction in prayer?
A. The whole Word of God is of use to direct us in prayer;[1] but the special rule of direction is that prayer which Christ taught His disciples, commonly called *the Lord's Prayer.*[2]

  [1] 1 John 5:14
  [2] Matthew 6:9-13; with Luke 11:2-4

Q. 107: What doth the preface of the Lord's Prayer teach us?
A. The preface of the Lord's Prayer, which is Our Father which art in heaven,[1] teacheth us to draw near to God with all holy reverence and confidence, as children to a father, able and ready to help us;[2] and that we should pray with and for others.[3]

  [1] Matthew 6:9
  [2] Romans 8:15; Luke 11:13
  [3] Acts 12:5; 1 Timothy 2:1,2

Q. 108: What do we pray for in the first petition?
A. In the first petition, which is, Hallowed be Thy name,[1] we pray that God would enable us and others to glorify Him in

all that whereby He maketh Himself known,[2] and that He
would dispose all things to His own glory.[3]

[1] Matthew 6:9
[2] Psalm 67:2,3
[3] Psalm 83:1-18; Romans 11:36

Q. 109: What do we pray for in the second petition?
A. In the second petition, which is, Thy kingdom come,[1]
we pray that Satan's kingdom may be destroyed,[2] and that
the kingdom of grace may be advanced,[3] ourselves and others brought into it and kept in it,[4] and that the kingdom of
glory may be hastened.[5]

[1] Matthew 6:10
[2] Psalm 68:1,18
[3] Revelation 12:10,11
[4] 2 Thessalonians 3:1; Romans 10:1; John 17:19,20
[5] Revelation 22:20

Q. 110: What do we pray for in the third petition?
A. In the third petition, which is, Thy will be done on earth
as it is in heaven,[1] we pray that God by His grace would
make us able and willing to know, obey, and submit to His
will in all things,[2] as the angels do in heaven.[3]

[1] Matthew 6:10
[2] Psalm 67:1-7; Psalm 119:36; 2 Samuel 15:25; Job 1:21
[3] Psalm 103:20,21

Q. 111: What do we pray for in the fourth petition?
A. In the fourth petition, which is, Give us this day our daily
bread,[1] we pray that of God's free gift we may receive a

competent portion of the good things of this life, and enjoy
His blessing with them.[2]

[1] Matthew 6:11
[2] Proverbs 30:8,9; Genesis 28:20; 1 Timothy 4:4,5

Q. 112: What do we pray for in the fifth petition?
A. In the fifth petition, which is, And forgive us our debts
as we forgive our debtors,[1] we pray that God, for Christ's
sake, would freely pardon all our sins;[2] which we are rather
encouraged to ask because by His grace we are enabled from
the heart to forgive others.[3]

[1] Matthew 6:12
[2] Psalm 51:1,2,7,9; Daniel 9:17-19
[3] Luke 11:4; Matthew 18:35

Q. 113: What do we pray for in the sixth petition?
A. In the sixth petition, which is, And lead us not into temptation but deliver us from evil,[1] we pray that God would
either keep us from being tempted to sin,[2] or support and
deliver us when we are tempted.[3]

[1] Matthew 6:13
[2] Matthew 26:41
[3] 2 Corinthians 12:8

Q. 114: What doth the conclusion of the Lord's Prayer teach?
A. The conclusion of the Lord's Prayer, which is, For Thine
is the kingdom, and the power, and the glory, forever.
Amen,[1] teacheth us to take our encouragement in prayer
from God only,[2] and in our prayers to praise Him, ascribing

kingdom, power, and glory, to Him.[3] And in testimony of
our desire and assurance to be heard, we say, Amen.[4]

[1] Matthew 6:13
[2] Daniel 9:4,7-9,16-19
[3] 1 Chronicles 29:10-13
[4] 1 Corinthians 14:16; Revelation 22:20,21

Other Related Titles from Solid Ground

In addition to the *Leather Edition of the Baptist Confession of Faith and the Baptist Catechism* we have published more than 350 titles since 2001. Some are as follows:

Farewell Sermons by Baxter, Brooks, Manton, Watson etc.
Robert Hawker's *Poor Man's Commentaries*
Scriptural Exposition of the Baptist Catechism
    by Benjamin Beddome
The Marrow of True Justification by Benjamin Keach
The Travels of True Godliness by Benjamin Keach
Gospel Sonnets by Ralph Erskine
A Body of Divinity by Archbishop James Ussher
Heaven Upon Earth by James Janeway
A Short Explanation of Hebrews by David Dickson
Commentary on Hebrews by William Gouge
Commentary on Jude by Thomas Jenkyn
Commentary on Second Peter by Thomas Adams
Commentary on the New Testament by John Trapp
The Christian Warfare by John Downame
An Exposition of the Ten Commandments
    by Ezekiel Hopkins
The Harmony of the Divine Attributes by William Bates
The Communicant's Companion by Matthew Henry
The Secret of Communion with God by Matthew Henry
The Redeemer's Tears Wept Over Lost Souls by John Howe

Call 205-587-4480 for a Free Catalogue

The Association of Reformed Baptist Churches of America

The Association of Reformed Baptist Churches of America was founded on March 11, 1997. On that day the first General Assembly met to establish a charter membership of 24 churches from 14 states. Since then we have grown to more than 75 churches and continue to expand by the providence of God. We invite you to inquire further on how your church can become a member of this national association.

Our association is recent, but our churches have been established many years in their communities and share a rich heritage that extends back to the Reformation. We encourage you to browse the various parts of our web site posted below and learn more about us!

Jesus prayed in John 17 for His disciples to be brought to complete unity so that the world would know that the Father sent Him. ARBCA is designed to advance Christ's kingdom by providing a fellowship in which churches of common confession may find mutual encouragement, assistance, edification, and counsel. We participate in cooperative efforts such as home and foreign missions, ministerial training, and publications, along with other such endeavors deemed appropriate by the Association.

There are many large cities and towns without a Reformed Baptist church. A number of churches are desirous of planting churches in these desperately needy areas. What one church cannot do, many working together can. ARBCA can assist local churches with their church planting efforts. ARBCA can also help churches seeking pastors and pastors seeking churches.

Reformed Baptists have a distinct theology and practice. Because of this, the Association plans to develop its publishing arm to meet the printing needs for Christ-centered, church-centered, and covenantally Baptistic literature. Look to the opposite page to see some of the material that is presently available from our Reformed Baptist Publications.

ARBCA
PO BOX 289, Carlisle, PA 17013
(717) 249-7473 • www.arbca.com

Reformed Baptist Publications

The publishing endeavor of ARBCA is directed toward the promotion of confessional Christianity and biblical churchmanship, in our Association and beyond. The following booklets are offered to assist our churches in establishing and maintaining biblical convictions in light of our common Confession, the Second London Confession of Faith of 1689. Our purpose is to help churches seeking to reform their ministries by the Word of God.

Unconditional Election - Earl Blackburn

What Is A Reformed Baptist Church? - Bill Payne

The Means of Grace - Earl Blackburn

Baptism & Covenant Theology - Walter J. Chantry

The Myth of "FREE WILL" - Walter Chantry

A Critical Evaluation Of Infant Baptism - Greg Welty

The Implications of the Lord's Supper - Dic Eccles

The Lord's Day - Philip Schaaf

A Tale of Two Associations - Dr. James M. Renihan

Missionaries Should be "Immersed" in Church - Walter Chantry

Paedoism Or Credoism - Richard Barcellos

The Lord's Day Still Is - John Giarrizzo

Why You Should Join a Church - Earl Blackburn

The Baptist Catechism

Call us at 717-249-7473

CPSIA information can be obtained
at www.ICGtesting.com
Printed in the USA
FFHW01n1836010818
47617845-51173FF